D0819948

ART CENTER COLLEGE OF DESIGN
3 3220 00242 4567

planet patio

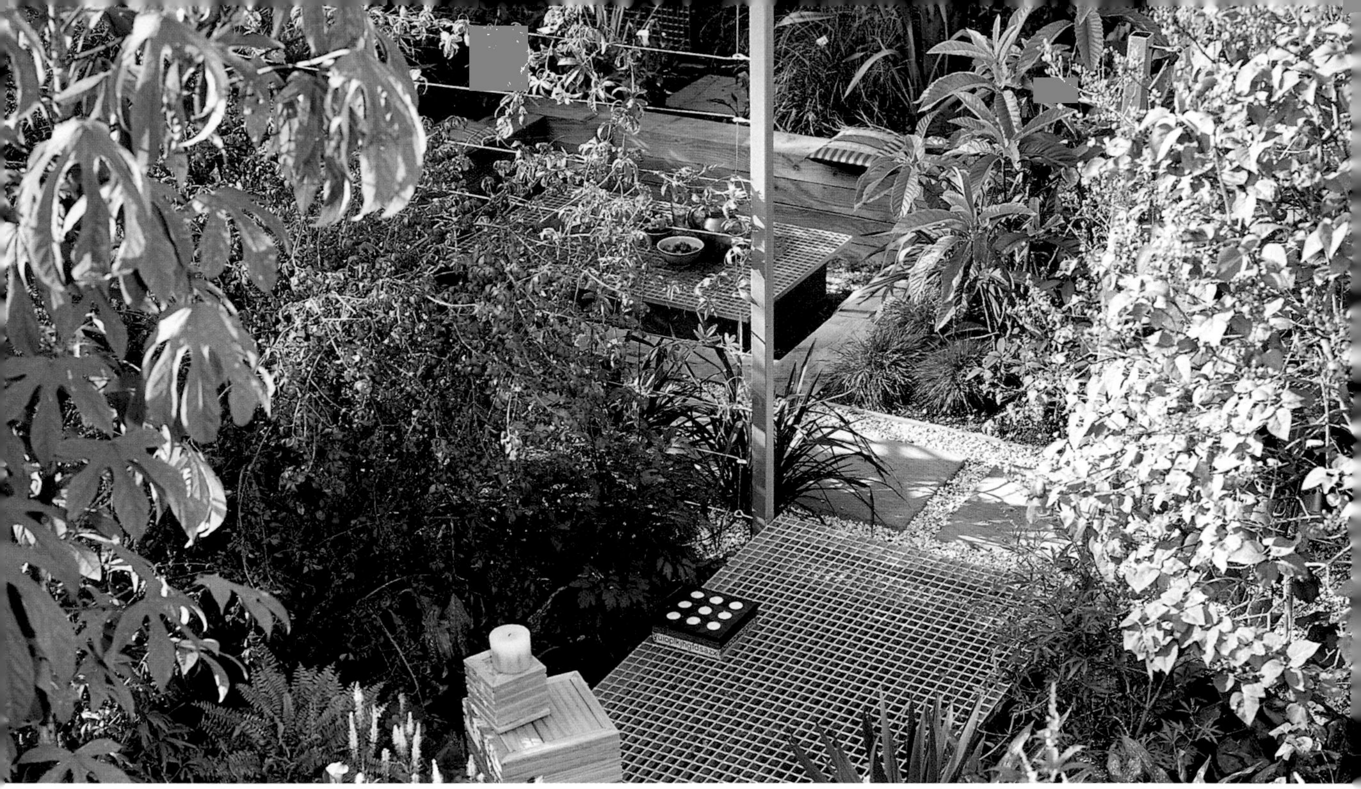

planet patio

stylish outdoor living

Diarmuid Gavin

BBC

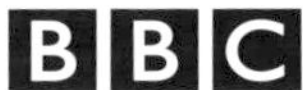

To Rebecca and Jack, with lots of love

contents

introduction

Planet Patio isn't a place – it's a state of mind. It stands for many things, but overall it's a place of escape, enjoyment, tranquillity, plants and design. Patio culture began in the twentieth century in North America at the luxury and fantasy end of gardening: Hollywood starlets cavorting around the pool in the Bel Air Hotel, Ron and Nancy Reagan with their all-electric house, Californian sunshine and Californian dreams. The patio was the place where things began to swing in the great outdoors.

Beyond the States, outdoor trends were much more restrained. Unless you were an avid gardener, fun wasn't a word much associated with Andersen shelters and vegetable patches. While American movies and sitcoms celebrated outdoor living, the British equivalents, such as *The Good Life* and *Terry and June*, delighted in crazy paving. But time and travel brought an appreciation of how Britain's European neighbours were beginning to live al fresco. All of a sudden anything seemed possible. Kylie and Jason and the soap opera, *Neighbours* revealed the lifestyle that we aspired to, and slowly but surely the garden as a territory was wrestled away from the traditional gardener and became open to all.

This fashion for outdoor living soon spread from the space just outside the back door to envelop the whole garden. Gardening and landscaping became the new rock'n'roll, but aspirational living didn't leave behind those with small spaces – the patio had become their new must-have accessory too. The perfect solution for small plots, a patio could be any shape, size, colour or texture; you could plant anything you wanted on it, in it, through it or around it, and you could even accessorise it to reflect your personal style and taste. Planet Patio became a world of choice.

And yes, sunshine isn't only for San Diego, a Walsall garden can bask in all that natural light has to offer and present a bold cacophony of colour. Likewise, just as chilling is as valid in Chester as in Cuba, so barbecuing doesn't have to belong to the residents of Ramsay Street – cooking fish over an open fire by the sea is a great way to experience the outdoors on your patio. Furniture, too, has moved on since the cast iron benches of the Victorian park – wood, glass, steel, plastic and acrylic are now all in vogue. Where garden containers used to mean stately urns, now they can be made of transformed copper boilers, aluminium ducting or even sections of clay pipe. Traditional gardens can develop new twists, as an amphitheatre of food drips around your paved plot or a beautiful tree grows through the centre of your dining table. Planet Patio is the place to explore.

Planning your patio

According to the dictionary, a patio is a paved area or courtyard adjoining a house. But, oh, how times have moved on. A patio can be anything you want it to be – just close your eyes and make a wish, and remember the rules have changed.

As with any design project, planning is the key to success. Putting some thought into your patio design at the start will make a big difference to the end result. First, establish the reasons why you want to have a patio – this will make it clear in your head how you are going to use the space and what you need from it. For many people a patio is a place with outdoor flooring on which to set a selection of furniture, but it can cater for many other needs too. If you are a sun worshipper, you'll want space to bask in an open aspect; if you entertain regularly, the space should be big enough for a large table and ten chairs; and if you love cooking, it should be planted with herbs and vegetables.

Often the patio will be designed as a section of a bigger garden; but for many people whose outdoor space is extremely limited, the patio may take up most, if not all, of your garden space. A patio need not be restricted to traditional garden spaces, it could also be built on a balcony or roof area.

Before you finalise your design, ask yourself some questions. As well as thinking about what you want the patio for, consider too how and when you are going to use it. Once you decide on this, think about where in the garden the patio should be situated to best meet these needs. Do you want a high- or low-maintenance garden – how much time will you have to spend working rather than relaxing in it? Is some form of shade required if the patio is in a very sunny aspect?

What style would you like – contemporary or traditional – and do you want this to be reflected in the materials you choose? You will need to consider the materials carefully if the patio has to link into any existing buildings or structures. Decide early on how you would like to divide the patio space between planting and hard surfaces, and consider if plants in pots or containers will play a key role. What accessories or extras should you include, and what services (such as water and electricity) will the patio need? Do you want built-in seating or barbecues, or do you have the storage space for less-permanent furniture? And, on a more practical and economic level, are you going to undertake the work yourself or employ a contractor?

Site and aspect

This is the main consideration for your design – where in relation to the garden as a whole are you going to site the patio? Sometimes the answer will be obvious. From a utilitarian point of view, a hard surface running across the back of the house is almost always required – if this links in with the best aspect (generally regarded as south-facing – when a house or garden faces the sun), the decision as to where to put the patio has already been made for you.

There are many advantages to locating a patio so close to the house, not forgetting the fact that you can throw open the doors for al fresco living – after all, it's easier to eat outside if your garden table is near the kitchen. On the other hand, many people live very busy lives, and the only time they are able to take advantage of the patio is after work on a summer's evening. In this situation you would probably want the patio to be halfway down the garden, or even at the end, depending on where the sun sets.

Placing your patio away from the house in a large garden, can make it a focal point in itself. A well-designed and constructed paving area can be a beautiful feature which, when viewed from the house, can entice you into the garden, and can also allow you to appreciate the house in relation to the garden, from a distance. You may even decide that your particular site requires two patio areas, like the 'Sea view' garden (page 104), with the main one near the house and another one taking advantage of the aspect.

Although it's unusual to have a patio in a front garden (because this site does not often afford the privacy and seclusion that many of us require), if the front of your house offers the best aspect, why not consider it? There's no rule either that says your patio has to be a wall-to-wall construction, it can melt into the garden, or be of various shapes, surrounded by plants. Don't be afraid to move away from traditional thinking and experiment with different ideas if they meet your needs and those of your garden.

Boundaries

Most gardens are surrounded by some sort of boundary, and in a really small plot this will be a significant part of your garden. But don't just think about the existing boundaries – you might decide you want a new fence or wall to separate off your patio area, or to create a link with the patio surface and form a more complete structural feature, or to provide privacy or shelter from wind exposure. A wall can also supersede existing garden barriers, forming a uniform background to your seating area. Walls can be built from a variety of materials and can contain a number of finishes – as the 'LA Story' (p26) and 'Sea view' (pp106–7) gardens demonstrate. Try to leave room for planting at the base of the front of your wall, as this will help to visually bed the structure into the garden.

If you are building a wall from scratch, make sure when siting it that you don't lose too much land or garden behind it, but also bear in mind that, while a small area behind the wall can make an interesting and mysterious space, a large area could become an inconvenient place to maintain. Like the patio, walls can be built to any shape. Check with your local planning office as to how near the boundary structures they can be placed and to what height they can go – generally this is 2.2 metres. Be aware that if your wall is above a certain height or length it may need inbuilt supporting pillars.

Materials

Not so long ago, it was easy to integrate an outdoor paved space into your surroundings because houses, outbuildings and boundary walls were mainly built from local stone, or readily available brick. If you wished to construct a paved surface, your options would have been limited to these materials and you probably would have chosen the local limestone or sandstone that everything else was made from. This was because the cost of transporting different materials was too great. Now, fortunately or unfortunately, this is no longer the case – a vast array of materials are widely available – including many which have originated in very different environments around the world.

Too much choice can create confusion – as a visit to any patio centre will quickly reveal – as indeed will the magazines, books and television shows, which continually present us with the next big thing in colour, texture, or material. In recent times, for example, this has been decking. You, however, have to decide what is right for your patio – what fits in, and what you can afford. From a style point of view, you might love the fact that decking is constructed from a natural material and easily links with the wooden flooring surface in your home. However, unless your site is open and sunny this could be the worst decision you make – a wooden deck can transform itself into a mouldy ice rink if not sited properly.

In recent years, many new concrete patio slabs have been developed to imitate natural materials such as stone or old-world cobbles – you can even get some that are designed to look like wooden decking. Your choice of material is often down to personal taste, but having a good knowledge of what's available and deciding what you really love will help enormously. My favourite will often be a plain, grey slab – something that isn't a garish colour and doesn't try to dominate a garden.

You may decide you want to mix and match – many people will build up designs using different coloured slabs – but, as a general rule, subtlety is the key to success and the fewer different materials used in the garden, the better. Combining paving and gravel can not only work very well (as in 'Viva al fresco' – p36), but can also cut down the cost of laying paving over the whole surface.

Comfort in the garden is an issue that is becoming increasingly important to people who value their leisure time. The idea of wandering barefoot through the garden is a very attractive one, but cold stone, or even coarse gravel and cobbles, can take away the romance – wooden decking could be the key here, or even outdoor underfloor heating!

The constant search for something new has led to experimentation with metal as an outdoor surface material. While its use can be beautiful and contemporary, it does have a limited application. Its obvious disadvantages are its susceptibility to changes in temperature – it can be very cold or very hot underfoot, and, in the case of metal grill, it is a strictly shoes-on, but no high-heels, material. Broad sheets of metal, such as stainless steel and galvanized aluminium, could also cause an enormous glare factor in the garden.

On the other hand, if implemented well, the possibilities of metal can be wonderful. If your garden space is extremely limited, you can use metal grill as a patio surface and underplant it with as many plants as you wish. In the 'Viva al fresco' garden, metal grill was used for flooring and also for a table, with beautifully fragrant chamomile growing through it. Using metal in the garden helps create a stylish, contemporary structure, as well as allowing you to explore a new relationship between plants and materials – it's very exciting.

Water

The sight and sound of water as you sit in your garden can create a magical and relaxing atmosphere, and there's no reason that you can't introduce water onto a small patio. A simple yet effective way of including a pond might be to sink an oak tub into the ground and surround it with planting, or just let it stand on its own on top of a paved area. For a more dramatic effect, the whole patio could be surrounded by a channel of water – creating a kind of island retreat.

One advantage of featuring flowing water in a garden is that it can mask irritating and disruptive noise by diverting your attention away from the racket, and towards its own, pleasing sounds. This can be worked into your design in many ways, through wall-mounted fountains, pumps in ponds, or rills snaking through your garden like miniature canals (such as those incorporated in the 'Japan' garden, p92, and 'Edible Eden', p74). Of course, with new technology there is no reason why you can't have water falling from a greater height, perhaps even down a glass wall on one side of your seating area.

Introducing water onto a patio can be a simple process, but it is one that requires careful planning in the early stages of your garden design. The main choices you will face will be whether you prefer running or still water, how big you want your feature to be, where you would like to place it and if you are going to incorporate marginal or aquatic plants.

If running water is required, you will need to introduce a pump, generally a submersible one, to circulate the water. This will involve employing an electrician to lay the necessary cables, a factor which, again, you should take into consideration early on in your planning, so that you won't have to dig up the surface later on. Although installing a very simple, still pond is not a complex operation, a full eco-system will need to be created to provide the water with oxygen, thereby keeping it fresh.

Of course, even shallow ponds can be dangerous for young children, so do bear this in mind when deciding on your water feature. Install a feature that is safe for children, such as one which stores its water in inaccessible reservoirs.

Hi-Tech

It's not long since our grannies would have been amused by the idea of gas heaters – for the outside – never mind inflatable furniture or plastic decking. But now so much more choice is available to create your perfect outside room.

For many people, the patio is a place for relaxing or entertaining in the open air, and commercial companies have quickly responded to the consumer's desire to make evenings in their gardens last longer. As a result, there is a wonderful array of outdoor lighting and other hi-tech equipment available. Don't forget that a lighting scheme can be entertaining as well as practical – it needn't just illuminate focal points in your garden or provide light over your dining area. With a bit of imagination, you can create a delicate, starry-sky effect with fibre optics, or even your own Saturday Night Fever disco paving, as in 'Lounge lizards' (p57), with lights twinkling underfoot.

If you do need to install electrical cables, remember to employ an expert, and get him to do the work *before* you lay your patio. However, don't despair if your hard surface already exists and you don't want to dig it all up again, because there are cable-free alternatives readily available for use outdoors, such as solar-powered or spike lights.

If your patio is going to be a place for entertaining, rather than a peaceful retreat from the modern world, you may want more extras than just lighting, and there is no reason why you can't take all the features of your indoor living-room, outdoors. Why not relax over dinner with some atmospheric music floating across the table? Or perhaps watch the big match in the sun while you turn the burgers on the barbecue?

Once again, make sure that any technological accessories you decide on are included in your plan and safely fitted. But don't forget, too, that although you may long for an exciting, entertaining patio, your neighbours may not have the same plans for their garden!

Colour

There are, of course, many other ways to add a stylish, contemporary feel to your patio without incorporating new materials or technology – colour can transform dull walls and fences, add drama and even subtlety, and disguise eyesores or highlight interesting features in your garden. Using colour in your garden has now become much more popular, and this is reflected in the rainbow of colours of outdoor paints and stains that are now available. However, don't go mad painting every surface in sight, remember – less is more.

Colours such as green and black work wonderfully in gardens to make unsightly sheds or walls disappear – brown can also help as a disguise, but otherwise it's not advisable in a garden because it doesn't provide any contrast. For bold, dramatic statements, consider blue – especially cobalt blue as used in 'Edible Eden' (p64), or dark aubergine, and, whatever the boys may think, pink looks brilliant in bright sunlight. Again, I wouldn't recommend using it as an overall colour, but when painted in blocks as in the 'LA Story' patio (p29), pink can be very rewarding and can bring a touch of West Coast America to your plot. Gold is becoming popular as a part of the current trend for Eastern-style gardens, but, as with red, apply it sparingly or it could dominate your garden.

So, colour can be a wonderful addition to your garden but it does work best in relation to planting: plants can tone down bright colours and, in return, colour can enhance the foliage or flowers of your plants. Of course, when talking about colour, we shouldn't forget the effect that plants themselves can create – either when planted as one colour or in a varied border.

Planting

For many people, plants make a garden, but it is really a personal choice as to how much or how little planting you wish to incorporate in your design. By now you will have decided whether you want containers or beds on your patio, and will have thought about how much time you have to spend working in the garden. These are factors that affect your choice of plants but, consider too the style of your patio and whether you want to grow your own produce, or whether you prefer a minimalist design with just one or two spectacular plants.

A trip to the garden centre can be inspirational, but it can also be very frustrating when it presents you with a mind-boggling array of plants. Don't be tempted to go for the ones that catch your eye first, think carefully about your planting plan and choose plants that are most suited to your plot. This is not as daunting as it sounds – just bear in the mind the aspect, soil and style of your garden before you go shopping. There's no point in investing in a beautiful *Agapanthus* if your garden is shady, susceptible to frost and has soil with poor drainage, or in buying a young *Magnolia*, only to watch it grow too big for a tiny patio space. Think about the look you want to achieve, and what suits your design.

Traditionally, pots and containers lend themselves to patios, but there are few rules here, and raised beds or borders can look just as good if carefully planned. Building raised beds gives you a larger container to work with, and lifting plants above ground level can make smaller plants look more impressive. Of course, containers don't necessarily need to be small, so think about your pots before you buy them: make sure they complement each other, as well as your patio, both in size and style.

Climbers can find a home in any garden, whatever its size, as they take up relatively little ground space. If you have an unsightly wall or fence, or just want to soften hard edges around your patio, planting climbers is a great solution, and if you select your plants carefully, climbers can also give all-year cover to an eyesore. Building a pergola and planting it with *Lonicera*, jasmine or even a vine can provide a cool, shady spot on a hot summer's day, and a fragrant patio on which to relax by night.

So, welcome to Planet Patio! Get out into the garden, take another look at your plot and start to imagine what it could be. No matter what size your garden, there's no reason why you can't have a patio to cater for your needs and wildest dreams. The gardens in this book demonstrate the versatility and scope of the patio, showing that you really can design your perfect outdoor space – be it a feast of organic planting or a stylish, minimal entertaining area – and bring Planet Patio into your own backyard.

LA story

From Hollywood poolside starlets to Venice Beach lifeguards, from David Hockney to the Beach Boys... the glamour of the West Coast of America has influenced British aspirational outdoor culture from the 1950s to the present day. But it's only now that we are beginning to realize that dull summers can be enhanced with a touch of the Californian dream.

The unique architecture that typifies design on the West Coast of America emerged very much for climatic reasons. The hot, dry climate was the classic environment for the development of the patio. In the 1920s, innovative architects, such as Frank Lloyd Wright and Irving Gill, pioneered ingenious concrete and cement-rendered architecture based on a few geometric modules and pre-cast units. This was suitable for Californian living for several reasons: it was the perfect material for maximizing space, reflecting light, exploiting the view of the sea and withstanding earthquakes! Large overhanging slabs of concrete provided specific areas of shade – perfect for poolside cooling off – but they also introduced a new building material.

West Coast architecture is also distinguished by its use of colour. The brightness of the palette reflects the healthy Californian way of life based around the sea, surf, fresh air and vegetation. The white of the concrete and glass reflects Californian light and space, blue reflects sea- and poolside water, while pink brings a touch of decadence – all set off by the lush green of exotic vegetation.

All these elements can be reproduced outside California to create the sun worshipper's perfect patio. It's the ideal extension to a stylish home and the ultimate hot spot on which to laze and unwind. Everything should be designed for absolute relaxation, from sun-drenched hardwood decking to low-maintenance desert planting. Style should be paramount, from sculptural coloured walls to sleek, slightly brutal poured concrete.

decking

Since making its jump from the boardwalk to the back garden, decking has proved to be the perfect flooring material for a small, open space. Decking is very adaptable in that it can be cut into almost any shape – so it's great for fitting into those awkward poky corners. It's relatively lightweight, so it's ideal for balconies, roof terraces or anywhere there is a load-bearing issue. Compared to other surfaces it's easy to lay and, with modern lifestyles becoming more hectic, it provides the perfect low-maintenance choice – doing away with lawn mowers and getting rid of high-maintenance borders certainly adds up to perfect stress-free gardening. As well as looking good, it's warm and soft underfoot, and its sleek and stylish durability will make the most mean and dingy of spaces into something long-lasting and magical.

Choices

There is an increasingly large variety of timber on the market to choose from. Your choice should be based on budget and aesthetic appeal, and the decision made as if you were choosing new flooring for your living-room. Consider all the general factors discussed on page 12 of the introduction when making this decision, for example, do you want to walk barefoot on it?

Hardwood timber is the luxury choice for decking – if treated well it will last a lifetime. The more familiar woods, such as mahogany and teak, have now been joined by a host of tropicals with such exotic names as ekki, bilinga, ipe and karri. The advantage of these tropical woods is that they are dense and relatively heavy, therefore making them naturally fire-resistant, free of knots and extremely durable. Hardwoods accept sealers and stains well, although their rich deep colours make staining seem unnecessary. Left to weather naturally, they develop a beautiful, soft, silvery sheen. Always check that your lumber comes from well-managed renewable forests – most dealers should be able to produce certification from the Forestry Stewardship Council.

Softwood timber doesn't mean that it's any less hard wearing than hardwood. It means that it is farmed from evergreen trees compared to hardwood deciduous trees. It's usually the cheaper choice but top of the range softwoods, such as western red cedar, share the same warm tones as hardwoods and look just as luxurious. A well-treated softwood deck will last up to twenty-five years. The decking boom has resulted in a large selection of quality durable softwoods being available off the shelf in just about any DIY store, either in traditional planks or in pre-formed squares – the really lazy and slightly more expensive option. Other softwood products include redwood, cypress, fir and pine, all characterized by a paler yellow colour and a more raw appearance.

Opposite: The clean lines of a hardwood deck contrast beautifully with the coloured sculptural walls.

Left: The rich colour of the South African karri deck enhances all the surrounding materials.

Above: Decking is the perfect outdoor material for an open sunny position. It is beautifully warm underfoot.

Construction

Building a deck is relatively simple but, as with all construction procedures, proper preparation is the key. Whatever your foundation, check you have adequate drainage, as moisture from wet ground or standing water can accelerate wood decay. Water also needs to drain off the top of the deck as well as from underneath it. If you are building your deck over grass, then cover it with heavy-duty sheeting, weigh it down with pebbles and pierce a few holes for drainage – this will prevent grass growing up between the boards. If you already have a patio in place, then, as long as it's level, you can simply build on top of it – the ideal urban solution.

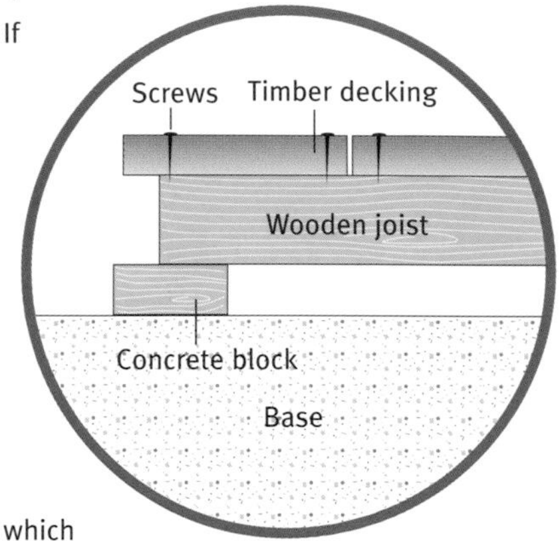

Posts sunk into the ground are essential if your foundation isn't level, or if you are building a raised deck, in order to support the weight of the deck and to provide an attachment for the underlying framework. Footings are basically large square posts (at least 100 x 100mm/4 x 4in) which are sunk into the ground onto a base of concrete.

Timber joists (150 x 50mm/6 x 2in) need to be carefully laid out to create the underlying framework which will support the finished deck. The heavier the timber, the closer the joists need to be spaced – position them too far apart and they'll sag or become uncomfortably springy. To be on the safe side, use a gap of 40cm (15in) as a rule of thumb between your joists. If you are building straight onto your existing patio and are concerned about drainage, you can lift the joists away from its surface with concrete blocks.

Boards come in a variety of lengths and widths. Have a good look at them before you actually fix them down, as the last thing you want is a knotty piece of timber right outside your French windows. Stagger your joints, so they alternate over your joists for a neat floorboard pattern.

Fixing your deck offers yet more choice. There is a host of specialist fixtures and fittings on the market which are suitable for decks, but the most important thing to remember is always to use galvanized or stainless steel screws – ordinary ones could ruin your whole deck with rust or corrosion.

Finish and Maintenance

The finish on a deck is important. Wood is a natural material and is weathered by water, sunlight and abrasion – even if you want to maintain the natural colour, it's advisable to apply a water-repellent preservative annually. If you prefer a more colourful option, you can buy specialist outdoor wood stains. Make sure they *are* specialist though – there's nothing worse than seeing the fruit of your labours peel off after a few days. If you do want to stain it, then choose a softwood timber, as it is more absorbent. It's a good idea to apply at least one coat of stain before you construct the deck so you get an all-round covering. Be warned though – however good the stain, it does wear off over time.

Beyond protecting your deck from damp, there's very little else to do – just apply the same principles as you do indoors, outdoors. Sweep the deck weekly to keep it clear from leaves and dirt, pull out plant growth from the base of posts and remove damaged boards immediately – avoid the rot setting in early and your deck will last you for decades.

Below: Good attention to detail and a neat finish is all important for constructing a beautiful and durable deck.

seating

Designing a beautiful patio is no good if you haven't got somewhere to sit and enjoy it. However small your plot, there must be enough space for at least one chair out there.

There are masses of different types of seating on the market, but it can be difficult to find something that suits your space perfectly. You could be adventurous and try making your own. Designing and building our own furniture is something most of us would never contemplate inside our homes, but outdoors the possibilities suddenly become more accessible and exciting.

Multi-function

If you do decide to build your own, then think imaginatively – can your seat be multi-purpose? In a small area, space is at a premium and storage is inevitably an issue. Look at what you already have in your garden; are there any existing walls that face the sun and the garden? If so, you can simply design a squarish, chunky bench out of block and render. Construct the actual seating base out of decking planks on hinges, so it can double as a lid; the inside of the seat can then act as a hidden storage area.

For sculptural and practical seating, concrete is a versatile material – you can mould it into just about any shape you want and paint it any colour. Some people think it looks wonderful in its natural raw form – slightly industrial and brutal, but a

perfect contrast to the warm, soft tones of timber. If you do go for the concrete option, think carefully – it is very permanent and once it's in place you'll have a job moving it.

Opposite: Apertures in a wall create windows for sunlight.

Below (left and right): A brutal block of concrete used in conjunction with softer materials and a background of colour becomes a sculptural delight.

Constructing concrete seating

To build your seating, first make a mould out of metal or wood – for larger constructions it is advisable to hire an expert who will use a specialist metal framework. Make sure the mould is well-braced and secured firmly enough to sustain a heavy volume, then fill it with a standard concrete mix – 4 parts ballast to 1 part cement. When the structure is completed, cover it to protect it from rain or damp and allow the concrete to set for at least twenty-four hours. You may find that once the framework is removed you will have little air pockets on the surface, but don't worry, as this all adds to the look.

walls + windows

Walls get bad press. There's something boring about building a wall and it may seem an odd choice for a small space, but once you stop thinking about walls just in terms of boundaries or screens, a whole new design possibility opens up. Walls can make real sculptural statements, perform as dramatic screens or divide a dull plot into something more interesting. Include some windows or openings in your wall and it can frame the view to the rest of the garden while also letting in some light, so that you can build closer to the house than you might have anticipated.

Practically, walls offer an ideal solution to hiding a multitude of sins, whether it be the pebbledash wall of a house or a wilderness garden beyond. They also provide a framework for you to garden within. Walls can be constructed out of brick, though lightweight breeze blocks are a cheaper and quicker alternative. Rendering your walls with outdoor plaster is a fairly specialist job, but worth the investment for a truly smooth and contemporary finish.

Opposite: A carefully positioned doorway will frame a view into the garden beyond.

Left: Contrasting colours used on rendered walls will brighten any garden throughout the year.

Below: At night drama is created by recessed lighting in a wooden seat uplighting linear 'windows'.

Construction

Building a brick wall can be a tricky and dangerous business if you have never constructed one before, so if you want anything other than a low level wall, it would be advisable to call in an expert rather than attempt it yourself.

If you do decide to build a small wall yourself, there are a few pointers worth remembering. Make sure your foundation is dug at least 60cm (2ft) deep and twice the anticipated width of the wall. Fill it with about 45cm (18in) of concrete (6 parts ballast, 1 part cement), so the first course of bricks, or half a breeze block width, can stay underground. Before you start building the wall, check the level of your foundation with a spirit level, and use pegs and a builder's line to set out the face of your wall. Lay out your first course of bricks using a 15mm (½in) spacer just to check that you've done your measurements correctly. Once you've mixed up a mortar mixture (6 parts soft sand to 1 part cement), trowel a 15mm (½in) layer onto your foundation, then apply about a 15mm (½in) layer between courses. Keep using your builder's line as a guide, and check with a spirit level every time you've got a couple of bricks down.

rockery 2001

If rockeries conjure up jaded images of middle-aged gardens from your childhood, then you wouldn't be alone. Surprisingly, this very suburban phenomenon originated from more exotic climes as a result of the late Victorian occupation of plant hunting – which was enjoying its most prolific period. Thousands of new species were being brought back from the far flung corners of the globe, and so the rockery was born out of the need to recreate these plants' original habitat of rocky terrain, poor soil and spot shelter at home.

During the twentieth century the rockery has become more of a style icon – most notably in the 1970s, with the craze for alpines and the ubiquitous dwarf conifer. It also provided a practical and sensible solution to the problem of what to do with excess topsoil. The arrival of readily available and cheaper plastics suitable for use as

Thelma and Louise planting style

If you're keen to take the Californian atmosphere to its maximum, then break the rules and move away from traditional alpine planting. Experiment with an arid desert feel using grasses and tough succulents.

GRASSES
Grasses are fairly subtle plants and although they bring shape and form, they are not going to add a blaze of colour to your patio. But planted next to a coloured wall or fence, such as the aubergine backdrop in this 'LA Story' garden, they can create a striking architectural display. The trick is to mix a variety of different colours and texture.

Carex buchananii is often mistaken for an ornamental grass, but is in fact a sedge that needs a damp position. Its densely tufted, hair-like, coppery leaves misleadingly give the impression of a burnt-out desert plant.

Briza media, or the quaking grass, has delicate flower heads that move in the breeze. The plant starts life green but soon bleaches to a faded parchment colour.

Miscanthus sinensis 'Zebrinus' or zebra grass, adds a bit of humour, with striking defined horizontal yellow stripes on narrow bright green leaves.

SUCCULENTS
Succulents are plants perfectly adapted to dry conditions and ideal for any small urban space where water is at a premium. They are usually identifiable by their fat leaves and thick skins, ideal for holding water. If you wanted to take the look to its absolute maximum, you could go for a comic-book cactus, such as the *Carnegiea gigantea*, but I'd only recommend this if you live in the Arizona desert and can wait for seventy-five years to see it grow to its potential.

Yucca gloriosa is a fantastic spiky plant that will eventually grow a short wrinkled trunk. Older specimens will flower every few years if grown on a hot site.

Sedum spectabile is a common British plant but can easily slip into an adventurous planting scheme. Most varieties are drought-resistant and actually prefer poor, dry soil. Be careful when picking your variety – some are rampant spreaders and could end up dwarfing your rockery.

Sempervivum 'Reinard', or the houseleek, is a peculiar little plant. Forming mounds of rosettes, its succulent leaves vary in shape and colouring and some are even cobwebbed for maximum ghost town appeal. Tuck a few into those really dry, rocky corners.

Grasses

Sedum spectabile

Yucca gloriosa

Sempervivum 'Reinard'

pond liners meant that homeowners in the 1970s found themselves part of another craze – for ornamental ponds. The topsoil excavated for these ponds conveniently heaped up and, with a few strategically positioned rocks, created a rockery that looked like a currant bun.

To create a rockery in a hard outdoor space, lift a few slabs or cut a shape into your decking to create a shallow bed. Excavate your foundation stone to a depth of 45cm (18in). Pick a few large smooth boulders that you can place in a single group and plant around. Always make sure that the rocks you use are quarried and environmentally friendly and have come from reputable sources. Alpines, succulents and grasses aren't too fussy about what soil they are in, so just use ordinary garden soil when planting them.

Opposite: A bed inspired by an Arizona landscape combines boulders with plants species such as Sedum, Yucca *and* Carex.

exotic planting

Over the past ten years the modern gardener has become more willing to abandon tradition and enter into tropical adventures. For years palms and ferns have been hidden and nurtured under glass, but the reintroduction of hardy varieties has meant they have been welcomed into our gardens. Some specimens need extra care and protection in the winter, but a covering of fleece or bubble wrap and a sheltered spot can help even the most tender and exotic of plants to grow on many patios.

Cordyline australis, or the cabbage tree, is a palm-like tree that starts off life as a large rosette of sword leaves and eventually matures into a trunk topped by foliage. Municipal parks and seaside promenades have long been characterized by their sub-tropical appearance among the marigolds and petunias. It's an exotic garden essential and can be found in traditional green, variegated or in a glorious deep purple.

Musa basjoo, or the banana plant, has large, thin, bright green leaves and is one of the least hardy of the outdoor exotics. These plants need to be sheltered, as the wind can rip through their foliage, but some bubble wrap or fleece will protect from winter frost.

Trees in pots

Just because you have a small space, it doesn't mean you can't think big in terms of planting. A lot of people shy away from using trees, but they can really give a feeling of maturity and grandeur. Provided they are well watered and fed, there is no reason why trees and large shrubs can't thrive in containers. Generally the pot should be twice the width and depth of the root ball, and if a plant is in an exposed site, keep it low down and well anchored. When choosing your tree, try to avoid fast-growing species, such as eucalyptus, as they quickly out-grow their pots. Always place your pot where you want it before you plant, so you won't have to drag heavy specimens around the patio.

Trachycarpus fortunei, or the windmill palm, is a magnificent tree, truly evocative of desert island peace and tranquillity. Its huge fan-like leaves give spot shade and are supported by a single shaggy trunk. Although it can reach 12m (40ft) in height, it is rarely seen over about 4m (13ft), so it is ideal for a limited space.

Olea europaea, or the olive tree, is usually associated with Mediterranean regions, where it has well earned its reputation as the queen of drought-resistant plants. It has beautiful foliage of narrow leathery grey green leaves which will eventually form a wide crown. If you're hoping for olives, you'll be waiting a long time – in cooler climes they are cultivated purely for their decorative charms.

Opposite top: Musa basjoo *(Japanese hardy banana) can be a surprising addition to British gardens. You may need to protect its foliage in winter.*

Opposite below: An olive tree, Olea europaea, *basks in the warm reflected light of the hot pink wall. In colder places it could be moved to a conservatory to overwinter.*

Left: A hardy palm, Trachycarpus fortunei, *planted in a large pot completes the exotic feel.*

extras

Lounging

No California-inspired patio is complete without the essential lounger. Ironically, although meant for relaxation, sometimes these loungers can appear to be designed for style rather than comfort, so the key to success is try before you buy. Don't be seduced by the latest fad or trend, opt for comfort first then think practically – do you have anywhere to store it? If not, then be prepared to treat timber models annually with a preservative. Finally, think style, there is a lounger out there to suit every sun-worshipper – from the sublime to the ridiculous.

Right: The wide range of loungers currently available, means you can now relax in style as well as comfort.

Opposite top: For those hot summer days in the sun, aloe vera is a wonderful, natural, after-sun treatment.

Opposite bottom: Lavender is famous for its aromatic relaxation properties, so plant it around your patio for the perfect lounging atmosphere.

Sun worshipper essentials

Lounging in the sun should be the ultimate relaxation experience and a time for pampering and self-indulgence. Unfortunately, this idyllic scene can be all too easily ruined if you are plagued by insects or fall victim to sunburn. But some clever planting can repel unwelcome visitors and produce your own supply of natural remedies.

Lavender is perfect for scattering in pots around your lounging area, as not only does it have wonderful aromatic relaxation properties, but at night it keeps moths away. Chamomile and eucalyptus are equally good at repelling mosquitoes, and peppermint and chrysanthemums are ideal for driving away ants, so try to work them into your plans for a dining area. And if you overdo the sun-worshipping, just break the leaves off an aloe vera plant and rub the sap directly onto your skin for a wonderfully cooling effect.

Viva al fresco

Patio passion kicked off in the early 1970s. Higher wages, shorter working hours and the birth of the package holiday introduced many people to the delights of the Spanish costas. For the first time, eyes were opened to the possibilities of outdoor living, and especially outdoor eating – a previously unheard-of pastime.

yuiopkjhgfdsazx

The humble suburban terrace soon became renamed the patio, a Spanish word bought back (along with the sombrero and the stuffed donkey) by tourists who wanted a smack of Spain in their homes. The aroma of food cooking outdoors, mixed with the heady scent of jasmine, set off a Channel-crossing trend...Viva al fresco!

Over the past thirty years, Britain's continental neighbours have moved entertaining outdoors onto a whole new plane. The big fashion centres of Europe reflect a passion for pavement living. Parisian cafés spill out onto the street and offer locals and tourists an open-air way of life. The British have been slow to adapt to this trend, partly because of the weather, but over the last few years, they've caught up with their European neighbours. Pizza parlours, bars, cafés and restaurants have all invested in the fashion for outside areas decked out with shiny steel furniture, giant canvas shades and fragrant planting.

And as a new attitude takes over communal areas, expectations are raised even higher when entertaining at home. But can a small patio space be transformed into a truly viable entertaining area? A party can mean many different things, but we all know that it's possible to cram dozens of people into the smallest room in the house if it's a really good party, so, of course, the same can be applied outside. The key is planning: how many people can you invite, do you want to eat, cook, stand around and chat or even have a bit of a dance? Once you have your list of requirements, with a bit of thought and care you can create the perfect party garden.

heavy metal

Metal is a material that we are used to seeing around us. It's been part of our industrial and commercial landscape for decades and, more recently, domestic variations such as stainless steel and galvanized aluminium, have started to take over our homes through hi-tech kitchens and bathrooms. There's something exciting about using metal, especially outdoors. Its sleek, hard elegance and reflective qualities make it a wonderful contrast to the softness of greenery.

Choosing your metal

Before you pursue the idea too far, remember the general considerations discussed on pages 8–9 and think carefully about the look you want to achieve, as this will have a huge bearing on which material you choose. Copper, with its shiny autumnal tones, will seem to melt into the garden, as its finish changes over time into a verdigris green. Stainless steel is expensive, but it is the most advisable choice because it weathers well, doesn't tarnish and lasts the longest. You do need to commission what you want from a specialist manufacturer, but the advantage with this is that you get it cut exactly to the size you want and you can choose which finish you prefer. Another option is mild steel; if you like a rusty finish, then this is an interesting choice – it will naturally decay over time but still last for decades, depending on its thickness.

Opposite: Metal grill makes a fantastic contemporary flooring in a garden which can be softened by underplanting.

Left: A table underplanted with chamomile will create a beautifully scented surface on which to serve dinner or drinks.

Metal is extremely adaptable and can be used in almost any part of the garden in a variety of ways and forms. It can be applied as wall-cladding, or in a mesh form to create light-enhancing screens and dividers, as solid backdrops or elegant trellis for plants, as giant planters and raised walkways or even for whole patio surfaces.

Grill flooring

An outdoor party needs hard surfaces for furniture and for people to stand around. Solid surfaces can look a bit stark, however natural the material, but both light and planting can be ingeniously introduced by using metal grill. Planting around and underneath a grill platform can soften the whole space, and these semi-shade conditions are ideal for lush ferns and hostas.

One advantage with grill is that you can place it almost anywhere. If you have a bit of old crazy-paving or a gravel patch you want to cover, then you don't have to worry about moving or levelling it – just place the new surface over it, and if you can see the old patio underneath, who cares? It all adds to the character. If you don't want to use grill for your main patio area, but like the idea of incorporating it, have it cut into walkways to link different areas of your patio.

There are disadvantages though. It's not cheap and not a DIY job: you will need to have your grill cut to size by a specialist metal manufacturer, and it then has to sit on a table structure of welded steel sections that have been rust-protected, and concreted into place. It's also not a comfortable surface for bare feet or high-heeled shoes!

Trellis has been appearing in gardens for centuries, both as a host for plants and as a garden divider – creating instant temporary or permanent boundaries and screens, or defining avenues and secluded areas. It is also very useful for covering ugly features, such as oil tanks or sheds. But even in a small space trellis can provide solutions to common problems. If you want to make a structural statement in your garden, trellis is an excellent choice as, even when covered with mature greenery, it will allow precious sunlight through where it could otherwise be limited. It can also help brighten up gloomy courtyard walls by allowing planting skywards rather than at lower levels, which in turn creates extra space in the beds for yet more plants.

Traditional

The most readily available trellis is the classically-inspired diagonal or square patterned timber panels, which can be bought in almost any size. Large panels can be used to construct a boundary with timber posts sunk into concrete footings, and small oblong panels can be added to the top of fence panels for extra height. Trellis is also an excellent way of complementing old brick walls.

When fitting trellis, don't attach it flush against the surface, it should be secured to battens so that air can circulate the plant. If you want a more original trellis, staple mesh to it or cut it into different shapes. It nearly always benefits from a coat of stain – traditional greens and blues work well, and black is excellent at helping the trellis melt away.

Coppice

Coppice wood is the thin section wood that has been cut from hedgerows, complete with bark. Unlike timber it hasn't been planed, processed or straightened and is one of the most natural and organic materials for outdoor construction. Coppice woods, such as willow and hazel, have been used for centuries in hurdling – weaving wood to form fences – but the ancient craft also works well for trellis. The final effect is beautifully delicate, but this is not a low-maintenance option. It's a living structure so it will need watering, and a shady spot is imperative, as it won't survive heavy wind-battering.

Metal grill

Metal grill used vertically as an alternative trellis gives a contemporary feel to your garden. As metal is substantially heavier than wood, each screen will need to be supported by steel rods fixed firmly into the ground – so creating fairly permanent features that should only be considered if you intend to stay put for a while.

Above: Metal grill used as a garden wall is customised with small rectangles of blue perspex. When backlit by the sun, the grill adds drama and colour.

Left: This diamond-shaped trellis is a traditional option for encouraging climbing plants, but it can be contemporized with a coat of paint or stain.

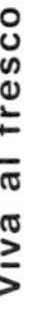

climbers

Put climbers into a small space and they will eventually cover boundaries and soften hard edges, turning dull walls and upright surfaces into living green walls. Considering the overall sizes that some climbers can achieve, they take up relatively limited floor space, providing you with as green an environment as you want, but still with room to breathe.

In terms of which species of climber to opt for, treat it as you would any other type of planting and consider all the factors of position, style, and requirements as discussed earlier (pp16–17). You can choose a really vigorous grower, such as *Parthenocissus quinquefolia,* or Virginia creeper, which will cover garages, balconies and even whole houses with not much encouragement. But most climbing plants are less rampant and can be confined to smaller supports.

Supporting climbers

Some climbers need a helping hand in getting started, such as netting or wire, while others have developed their own methods of support as they evolved to scramble over or up other plants in their search for sunlight. Twining plants, such as honeysuckle,

Right: If you like the idea of using metal, tension wire can provide an excellent support for climbing plants. You will need steel posts to withstand the force of the tension. Choose fairly rampant climbers to cover it and attach them with wire – as the metal provides a more subtle support than traditional trellis. The advantage with wire is that it lets in the maximum amount of light and will form more delicate dividers than heavier structures.

support themselves by twisting and turning around trellis or trunks and branches. Other species, such as vines, support themselves by growing tendrils that literally coil themselves around supports. They do need a little help to start off with, but should then support themselves quite easily. Others don't have to be supported at all and will attach themselves directly onto walls with adhesive pads or aerial roots. The most famous of these in this part of Europe is ivy, which will cover anything it comes into contact with. For a party garden, big and blowsy colour is a must, but the deep green of English ivy can be a perfect backdrop.

Climbers are often planted in dry areas of the ground, such as at the base of stone or brick walls, so it is a good idea to dig a hole 20cm (8in) away to ensure the plant's roots are in more moist soil; then lead it back to its support with a bamboo cane.

Favourite patio climbers

There is an overwhelming range of climbers available for all areas of the garden, but here's a selection of my favourites for a patio space. Some of these are just easy on the eye, but others also help create a balmy, scented atmosphere for your patio.

Passiflora caerulea, or the common passion flower, is a fast-growing evergreen climber with beautiful white, pink-blushed, unusual flowers that unfortunately don't last for very long. It favours a well-drained, poorish soil and a sunny position, and is also suitable for growing from containers. Height: 10m (30ft).

Hydrangea petiolaris is a tough and vigorous plant that does well in most sites, although it favours a west-facing position and a moisture-retentive soil. It does take a while to establish, but will eventually develop into a thick mass of green foliage and white flowers. Height: 15-18m (50-60ft).

Lonicera periclymenum 'Serotina', or Late Dutch honeysuckle, is one of the most flagrantly fragrant of the climbers. These twining plants are slightly disorderly, get tangled easily and are vulnerable to blackfly and mildew. But they really are worth persevering with, as their scent is unrivalled. Prune every spring to one third to the ground and keep their roots well out of sunlight. Height: 7m (23ft).

Roses are enjoying a resurgence in modern gardens and a rambling mass of sweetly-scented roses is bound to bring out the romantic in anyone. There is a colour and a scent to suit everyone.

Rosa 'The Garland' is a richly fragrant Victorian rose with an abundance of small, creamy flowers.

Rosa 'Guinée', deep velvety red, has a luxurious appearance and heady scent. Like many roses, *Rosa* 'Guinée' generally likes a sunny south-westerly aspect

Rosa 'Albertine' is a favourite pink rambler distinguished by its combination of dark and pale pinks. It produces a richly fragrant scent.

Clematis is unsurpassed among climbers for their long period of flowering, different shapes and colours and tolerance to just about any site or aspect. *Clematis montana* produces an abundance of white and pink flowers that provide a dense mat of colour, ideal for covering eyesores. Height: 7-12m (23-40ft). *Clematis* 'Jackmanii Superba', on the other hand, makes more of a singular statement with wonderful deep, velvety purple leaves. Place it somewhere it doesn't get lost among other less show-off blooms. Height: 3m (10ft).

Passiflora caerulea

Lonicera periclymenum

Rosa 'Albertine'

Clematis montana

extras

Barbecue

The actual word barbecue means 'large wooden or iron framework for smoking or broiling' or 'an open-air party at which animals are roasted whole'. Modern barbecues developed in the United States in the early 1700s but it was not until the 1950s that America went barbecue crazy. It was also at about this same time that men were emancipated from culinary obscurity and became King of the backyard feast. As men typically pursue anything with gadgetry or gizmo, the barbecue market has responded by manufacturing a barbecue suitable for any wallet or appetite, confirming what we have known all along – men are mad about fire.

There is a wide variety of barbecues available in different sizes and shapes to suit the needs of yourself, your garden and your storage space. Personally, I prefer barbecues that can be moved out of the rain or out of the way when they are not needed – built-in barbecues can look very sad and abandoned when they are not in use.

Barbecue bonanza

Disposable: **If you're a barbecue novice, you could try a disposable model that you can buy in any supermarket. It offers a no-frills approach for no-frills food, but it's quick and cheap and there's no clearing up afterwards.**

Portable barbecue: **You could go up in the world with this sexy beast. Each one comes in the same chrome finish and features these handy legs. It looks good and, with care, will give great results.**

Mountain Smoker: **The smooth clean lines disguise a fiery animal waiting to get out. It looks a bit like a Dalek, but it won't exterminate your food. It works by heating water to boiling. The steam mixes with woodsmoke to give a unique flavour.**

Sunshine Legend: **If you're holding a big party, the Sunshine Legend is for you. It's quick and easy as it has a gas grill, but the downside is that it won't give your food that distinctive barbecue flavour.**

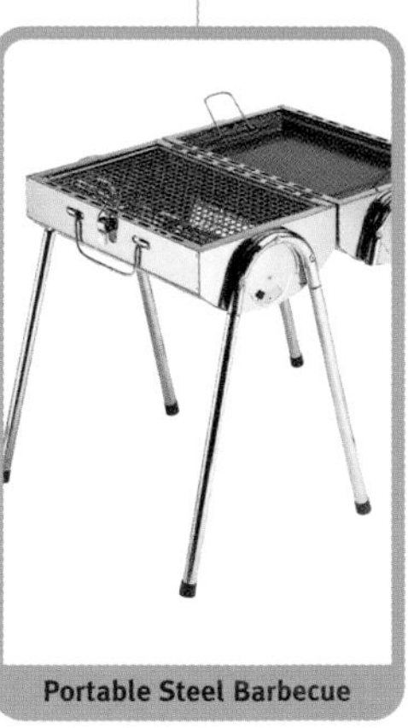

Portable Steel Barbecue

Mountain Smoker

Sunshine Legend

Seating boxes

The perennial problem at any party is where to seat everyone, and, when they've gone, where to store the seats. Patio tables and chairs can be pretty boring, as well as taking up a lot of space.

An ideal solution is to create seating boxes out of standard decking planks. Be adventurous: make them in a variety of sizes and literally scatter them around your patio. Then when everyone's gone, stack them up and you can have your very own sculptural feature.

- Cut the decking wood to the required length, with a 45° mitre at both ends . The amount of pieces will be determined by the size of the box and also by the width of the deckboards.
- Glue and nail the corners together to make square frames (1).
- Stack the frames on top of each other (2)
- Fix batons to the internal corners to hold the frames together (3). Finally, fill in the open ends with square-cut boards.

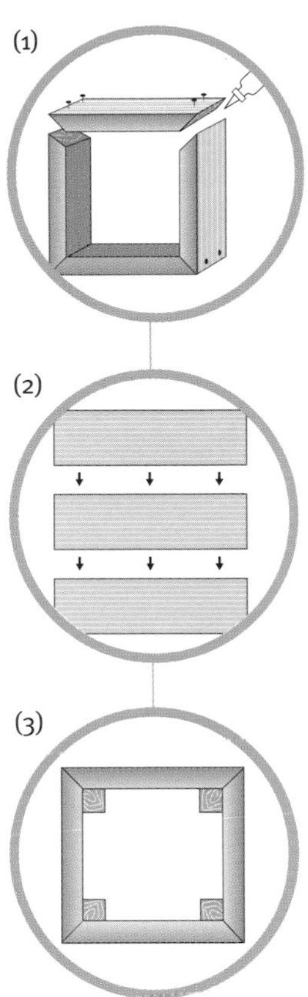

Opposite: Mobile barbecues are a great idea for British summers as they can be easily moved under cover when the rain sets In!

Left: Smaller versions of the wooden seating boxes can be constructed as tables or decorative objects for your patio.

Lounge lizards

We've long since got away from the Victorian idea of having different rooms closed off within the house and the parlour being kept for special occasions. Fifty years ago, open-plan living began to invade our domestic spaces, but only now are we celebrating the idea of a garden as a room outside.

Modern living can require many things of a garden. People have varied and complex lifestyles, so the option of the garden as an outdoor living-room – a place of relaxation or fun – has become increasingly appealing. As inside the house, the garden 'lounge' has to be multi-functional and quite often satisfy the needs of several individuals – offering a place to chill out on your own and read a book, or listen to music, or perhaps somewhere to sit, chat and eat in an intimate group, or a social space where you can have fun late into the night in an atmosphere enhanced by mood lighting.

On the other hand, your outdoor room can be your garden room – that place where you indulge in the traditional hobby of gardening, nurturing and tending plants.

In terms of style, the outdoor lounge is particularly suited to an urban environment. In more rural areas, an atmosphere can be enhanced by open vistas, acres of greenery, birdsong, clear skies and maximum light. City-dwellers, by contrast, invariably have brick walls, industrial landscape, shadow and often a hum of traffic. Here a truly modern statement can be made: hi-tech materials, uncompromising planting and state-of-the-art lighting can all come into their own to create an urban alternative with equally effective pockets of relaxation or entertainment. Fun can be had in mixing and matching styles. You might enjoy contemporary materials, for example, but might also love to bring a bit of traditional planting into the mix. You decide on your favourite recipe – old and new can work together in a very harmonious way.

turf's up

For as long as people have been creating gardens there has been lawn. Even though it had been around since medieval times, its use was not really celebrated until Capability Brown brought the lawn into its own. He removed the formal gardens of the seventeenth century to make way for sweeping swathes of grass that ran from the front door to the landscape beyond. So, why are today's gardeners still so fond of lawn? It's a soothing and tactile surface and, once established, surprisingly hard wearing. The lawn is the rug or roll-out carpet that sets the plants off or, indeed, links all the garden features together.

The fact that you have limited space is no reason for not introducing lawn. On the other hand, lawn, like any other outdoor flooring, has its pros and cons. It may provide instant gratification and thrive in a European temperate climate, but it isn't a low-maintenance option. If you don't have anywhere to store a mower, or would have to drag it up several flights of steps, then turfing wouldn't really be worth exploring.

Creating an instant mini-lawn

Consider carefully whether your site is suitable for turf. There are two things to bear in mind: do you have adequate sunlight, and is there sufficient drainage? Constant shade and lack of drainage can result in moss invasion and damp patches. Think about the

type of design you would like. Be adventurous – turf is easily manipulated, so think about S shapes and circles as opposed to boring straight lines. Steep slopes needn't be a problem any more, as modern mowers will let you mould your lawn into hills or up banks and still maintain them.

- Prepare your site. If you are laying turf onto good topsoil, then take time to remove rubbish and stones, and dig over to a depth of at least 23cm (9in).
- More preparation is needed if you are creating a raised lawn, or an area from scratch onto subsoil. Spread a layer of rubble on the subsoil and press down. Add a layer of grit or coarse sand, then replace the topsoil.
- Mark out your site, using string and pegs for straight lines, or spray paint or garden hose for curved shapes.
- Roll out each strip of turf, butting all sides closely together and gently patting down after each roll. Start your second row halfway down the length of the first, so all your ends aren't together in one line. Brush in a good loam mix.
- Once the whole area is laid, define your finished shape by cutting the turf with a sharp knife or a half-moon cutter.
- Water heavily and, however tempting, try to keep off it for at least seven days.

Opposite: A small circular lawn enclosed by a rendered-block mowing edge makes a perfect 'rug' in your garden.

While laying a lawn – whether by the traditional method of seeding or the more modern, instant, and expensive laying of turf, is relatively easy, maintaining lawn to the desired level of finesse can be fairly tricky. The secret of a good lawn is in its foundations, so if you get the preparation right at the start, your maintenance will be immeasurably easier.

A good base of topsoil is a necessity – a least 20cm in depth – it doesn't have to be rich in food, but it should be free draining. Avoid compaction by making sure that heavy machinery does not cross the prepared site. The best maintenance plan for any lawn is regular mowing. The first cut, once it has started growing, should be undertaken with the lawnmower blades set quite high. Mowing prunes the grass plants, encouraging them to develop side shoots, as well as keeping weeds at bay by chopping off new growth. Don't set your blades too low when mowing an established lawn, or you will shave the grass and create bare patches which will soon be colonised by moss and weeds. Some weeds, such as daisies and *Helexine*, seem to thrive under the constant caressing of the lawnmower. Although larger weeds can be taken out by hand, the more stubborn or elusive may need to be treated with either a selective or general weedkiller.

Your lawn will demand attention throughout the year. Prepare for the winter by scarifying and spiking. Scarifying, with a spring tine rake, removes built-up debris (thatch) from the base of the grass plants. Spiking alleviates compaction and allows for good air circulation and improved drainage. An autumn lawn feed sprinkled in September or October will toughen the roots, while another high nitrogen feed in the spring should green up your outdoor carpet for the summer months.

hi-tech

A lounge is a space that we can use day and night, all year round. The garden, on the other hand, has traditionally been somewhere that we only venture into occasionally, weather permitting. But we're beginning to ask for more from our gardens. Because it is our leisure time that we spend outdoors, we want to make the most of our plots whenever we can. And, as we are now also willing to make a financial investment in our gardens, the commercial sector will suddenly offer us with any amount of gadgetry and gizmos – from outdoor heaters to beer coolers.

Outdoor entertainment

Our desire to make full use of our internal entertainment centres outdoors has been fuelled by images of parties by the pool and on beaches. Sometimes we desire our outside space to be a tranquil and relaxed retreat – a place that isn't tainted by technology. However, at other times we may want to indulge in images, sounds and

effects which, up to now, have been alien to our garden spaces. Televisions, videos, projectors and stereos are all feasible options if they are installed and housed properly in water-tight constructions – the key is to seek advice from an expert who is used to working with outdoor electrics. Used carefully, these hi-tech devices can be an occasional, beneficial addition to our lifestyles; used rashly, they can be a social annoyance. Always remember that although you may be ready to embrace the outdoor lounge, your next-door neighbours may be more passionate about pruning and propagating than hearing Saturday's match in stereo.

Whether it's Pavarotti or The Pretenders, a favourite serenade in an open space is wonderful to hear, or beaming a classic movie such as *Gone With The Wind* across the garden onto a white sheet can turn a social evening into a real occasion. Even piping the sweet song of the blackbird into an outdoor space where it is never usually heard can add something extra to a leafy city garden – and, you never know, it might even attract some curious real friends. But if you just want atmospheric light rather than sound, then using projected light, whether it be an oil lamp scattering groovy images onto foliage and flowers, or even a shimmering curtain of fibre optic lights – can create a sense of magic.

Above: A full range of contemporary outdoor accessories are now available, so your garden furniture can reflect your personal style.

Opposite: Fibre optic lighting, used underneath concrete slabs set with blue glass lenses, adds real excitement to a city space.

Lighting

Regardless of their site or aspect, gardens completely change character throughout the day as the sun moves around it then finally sets. Lighting the garden can be motivated by practical or aesthetic considerations; reactor lights are ideal burglar deterrents, whereas spots and spikes can identify pathways and ponds for safe access through your plot. But lights can also be used purely for their entertainment value – to illuminate and transform your patio into an enticing and enchanting place to spend your evenings.

The requirements for lighting are different depending on whether they are for the inside or outside. Inside the house you're lighting an enclosed box, where the light is restricted and cannot escape, so it's easy to create different moods. Outside, on the other hand, a balance needs to be sought between dramatic shadow effects or bland over-lighting.

Absolute care should be taken when installing electrics to power lights, but as a rule of thumb:

- Always employ a qualified electrician.
- Before embarking on your overall garden design, plan your lighting carefully so that cables can be concealed without having to dig up the newly-laid turf or patio.
- Make sure any cable you use is steel-wire armoured.
- Outdoor power points should be covered and designed specifically for exterior use.
- Remember to fit a circuit breaker, which will cut off power in case of an accident.

What's available

Until relatively recently, the market was limited, but now dozens of products are available to suit every taste and budget – even offering different coloured lights to create dramatic or fantasy effects outdoors. Consider the choices carefully, because designing an exterior lighting scheme can be difficult to get right and easy to get wrong. Decide on your priorities, whether aesthetic or practical, and consider the moods you want to achieve.

Spike or spot lights are the most common option and have recently become available in contemporary and futuristic styles. Their advantage is that they can easily be stuck into the soil and pivoted to light up walkways and garden features, or even to underlight dramatically-shaped plants.

A solar-powered lamp can generate about four hours of light from the sun of a bright day, and sensors ensure that it doesn't stay on all the time. Solar lighting does away with all the wiring and the cost of an electrician, but on persistently cloudy days you may run the risk of a faintly-lit garden.

Floodlights are useful for displaying large features or buildings and, if carefully placed, can create drama at night out of nondescript walls or buildings.

Neon can bring a real touch of excitement to a garden. It's not that expensive, but the lights do need to be fitted by a specialist and can be a bit fragile. 'Nearly neon', or neon-style lighting is housed in flexible plastic cable which is much safer and easier to handle than the traditional stuff.

Fibre optics is a wonderful innovation that is beginning to reach its full potential in the domestic garden. Light is projected along glass fibres as fine as human hair, through strands of cable that look like black spaghetti. These cables can be bundled together but carry no dangerous electricity or heat. To use properly, the cables should be carefully positioned so as not to be obvious during the day. At night, their

Left: Blue glass adds colour and interest to a plain concrete patio surface.

pin-pricks of light create a dramatic effect. Colour wheels can be added to the projector box to give an ever-changing rainbow effect. As they are flexible, they can be manipulated and positioned exactly where they are needed. And while they are not practical for providing broad areas of light, their entertainment effect can be magical and startling. Once fitted they're virtually maintenance-free, with only occasional attention needed for the light source.

Disco flooring

The ability of a flat patio to be anything other than simply a hard outdoor surface is not obvious at first. However, in one of those unforgettable music video moments, Michael Jackson caused the paving slabs of New York to illuminate just by prancing about on them. Glass and concrete flooring has long been available, having been developed initially as a practical solution to basement lighting for shop cellars. Outside, at night, light shining through the frosted glass from below offers a hint of warmth inside, whereas indoors, floor space lacks the capacity for cavities for illumination.

However, things can be very different outside, and glass block paving has made a glittering transition into the garden. Constructing a patio out of these glass blocks is not a task to undertake lightly – it is serious industrial flooring and a monster to put down. The actual floor consists of pre-cast concrete slabs with circular or square glass lenses of varying colours, which are raised over a steel or block frame. A depth of 30cm needs to be kept clear for the fibre optic lights, to be set in a grid system pointing up at the individual glass lenses, so illuminating the space. The projector blocks for the fibre optics should be housed separately in a dry and accessible space for occasional maintenance. If you don't like the idea of coloured glass, why not try instead the combination of a colour wheel and clear glass lenses, which can also create the perfect disco flooring with a multi-coloured, Saturday Night Fever, ever-changing effect.

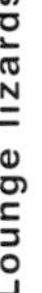

architectural planting

Architectural-style planting has become popular among gardeners. The term 'architectural' can encompass plants and planting combinations that bring real shape, form and texture into a garden. Cordylines, bamboos, cannas and bananas have very distinctive bowl-shaped foliage, and can be used in combination with the more feathery greens of ferns and grasses. You can experiment to create a lush cascade of striking foliage, or a minimalist statement using a solitary specimen. The secret is in creating a pleasing picture by combining different colours, textures and shapes.

Opposite: Dicksonia antarctica *and* Cordyline australis, *both plants with bold foliage, help to soften a highly structured garden.*

Below: Cortaderia selloana *(pampas grass) can be planted in beds or even in containers in smaller spaces.*

Dicksonia antarctica, or the Tasmanian tree fern, is king of the architectural style and an absolute 'must-have' for a modernist or subtropical planting scheme. It towers over all other planting with its tall, stout fibrous trunk and the sheer magnificence of its evergreen canopy of delicate lacy fronds that can reach up to 2–3m (6–10ft) in length. Surprisingly, this dramatic plant is relatively low-maintenance. Direct sunlight isn't a major requirement, but shelter is.

Phormium tenax, or New Zealand flax, is spectacular for its dramatic foliage, in this case, sword-like leaves that jut into the air. This species comes in an abundance of varieties and colours, from smooth grey to green to deep purple. It can grow up to 3m (10ft) and spread to 2m (6ft), but if you have less space or only want containers, you can get small varieties, such as 'Dazzler', that grow to only 90cm (23in). This has beautiful bronze leaves with red and orange tips. These plants like sunlight and shelter and thrive in mild southerly gardens or sheltered city spots. Although many varieties are winter-hardy, they should be protected in freezing spells with a covering of fleece or bubble wrap.

Cortaderia selloana, or pampas grass, has been long associated with suburban 70s gardens, but it really looks best set against vast acres of rolling lawn. Its leaves are razor-sharp and it produces plumes of white to faintly pink flowers very late in the year. Propagate by division. Pampas grass is very difficult to remove when it is established in a bed, but it is a dramatic plant that looks good either when given plenty of space, or when in a container.

Cordyline australis, or New Zealand Cabbage Palm, is a bit tender to frost, so not ideal everywhere but it is great for creating a tropical look. Perfect for patios, it is a small tree usually forming a single trunk with several branches, each topped by a large, dense mass of long, purple, sword-like leaves – a bit like a phormium. A great mass of creamy-white flowers is produced in big bunches in early summer. Grow in fertile, well-drained soil and full light or partial shade.

Gunnera manicata, or giant prickly rhubarb/poor man's umbrella. If you want a plant that really makes a statement, then look no further than gunnera. But you do need adequate space for this plant, as its outlandishly large leaves – up to 1.5m (5ft) across – can dwarf plants and places. It has compound flower heads in summer, which give a cone-like outline. It likes moist and rich soil, semi-shade, shelter from wind and a position in or beside water. It's not completely hardy in cold winters – the trick is to protect its crown by covering it with its own dying leaves.

cottage planting

Initially, cottage gardens were primarily functional and supplied the dweller with fruit, vegetables and herbs. Over time, wild flowers were introduced to these plots and soon plants were being cultivated solely for their flowers and fragrances. Plants were propagated by cuttings and division and soon whole communities were helping to develop a rural garden style.

In modern times the confusion and profusion of blooms in a cottage garden has become the stereotypical essence of the English garden. Boundaries are less defined and borders transform into a constantly changing palette. Despite the appearance of chaos, however, the ingredient that all these gardens share is the love and dedication of an older generation of gardeners – it is this quality that is the most difficult to replicate.

The majority of planting is made up of herbaceous perennials that vie for attention with each other during the summer months. In winter the plots can grow bare as flower and foliage die away, so planting evergreen shrubs, such as *Buxus sempervirens* or *Choisya ternata*, should ensure that the garden is truly mixed, retaining all year interest.

How to plant a herbaceous border

The technical definition of a herbaceous plant is that it does not form a woody stem, which means that many of them won't be there all year round, as they die down in winter. Traditionally, the cottage border would have relied on herbaceous plants only, but now the trend is to have mixed shrubs, using evergreens to form a skeleton background throughout the year – this also makes the border easier to maintain. Many people regard herbaceous gardening as real gardening, but don't let this put you off – this doesn't mean it is a really high-maintenance option. However, soil preparation is essential for herbaceous plants, as they are heavy feeders, so be sure to dig in plenty of well-rotted manure. As they mature, many plants will be need to be staked – unless they are planted fairly tightly together, in which case they can support each other.

The advantage of herbaceous plants is that there is a massive range available and such a variety means that great fun can be had in devising the correct scheme for your abode. Choose specimens that suit your plot, there's a herbaceous plant for every situation – sun, shade, dry or moist – and experiment with colour, foliage texture and different heights.

Opposite: Cottage garden plants are equally at home when planted in traditional borders or in contemporary containers, and look wonderful mixed with more dramatic plants.

Cottage planting favourites

Designing a cottage garden today allows you to experiment with your planting scheme. By all means use traditionals, but don't be afraid to intersperse a few modern, dramatic plants. Here are some cottage garden favourites which will give your borders the essential range of colours and heights.

***Alcea*, or hollyhocks, are probably among the most affectionately viewed of the shortlived perennials and more than any other species are the archetypal flowers from grandma's garden. Grown for their tall spikes and dancing heads they can be found in almost every colour in rosettes and double-headed flowers.**

***Pelargoniums*, or geraniums , are probably the happiest plants. They fall in and out of fashion but never fail to bring colour and a smile, whether in beds, containers or hanging baskets. They need warmth and sunshine, or else their appearance is all too fleeting. Hardy trailing geraniums are ideal planted at the feet of specimen plants, while the delicately-scented varieties are good for kitchen window boxes.**

***Hostas*, or the plantain lily, are used to great effect in the traditional herbaceous border or contemporary designer gardens. Available in dramatic ranges of foliage, from variegated blues to bright yellows and greens, they are hardy and need little care but, as yet, no one has really discovered the perfect way of keeping the snails off!**

Other cottage favourites ...
Other must-haves to bring colour, scent and shape to your borders are: *Dicentra spectabilis* (bleeding heart), *Digitalis purpurea* (foxglove), *Nepeta faasserii* (cat mint), *Rudbeckia fulgida* var. *deamii* (black-eyed Susan), *Lobelia*, *Euphorbia*, *Astilbe*, *Salvia* (sage) and *Hebe*.

Geranium

Hosta

Rudbeckia

Sage

extras

Relaxing outdoors

They're comfortable, they're portable and they're back – the new generation of bean bag is designed for outdoor living.

Silver bean bags— first it's a scatter cushion, now it's a chair. Vacuum-pack bean bag – this bag actually moulds to the shape of your body.

Vacuum packed bean bag chair — this amazing chair forms to your body when you sit in it, then retains it's shape

Inflatables— they're cheap, they're fun and, best of all, if they burst you can just buy another!

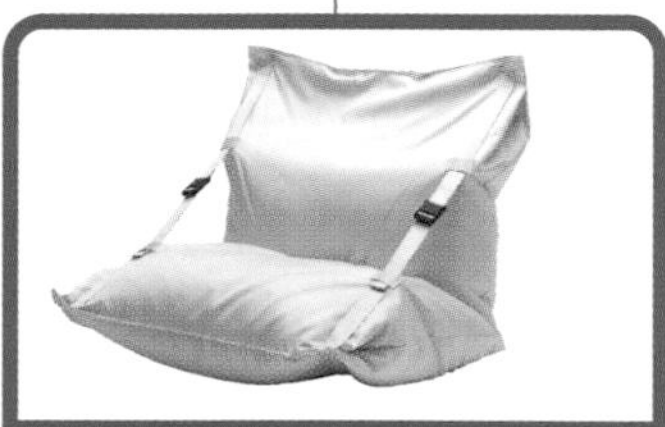

Scatter/bean chair

Vacuum packed bean bag

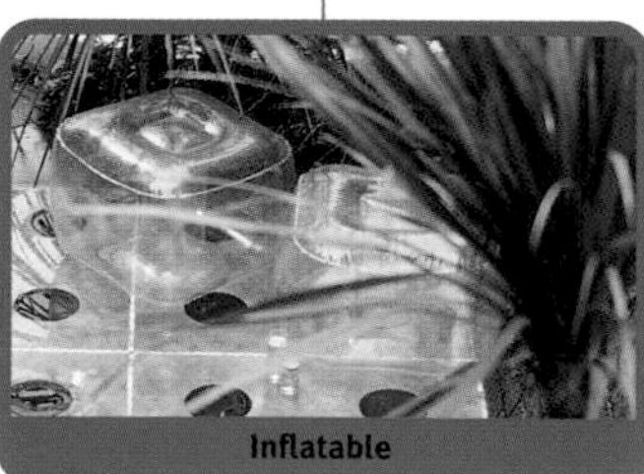

Inflatable

Get comfortable

It's difficult enough to find the perfect indoor sofa on which to relax, but add outdoors into the equation and the search becomes quite a challenge. What do you put in this outside room to really make it feel like home? Plastic or wooden patio seating is very practical, but if we crave the creature comforts of the lounge, we need something we can really sink into. There are now a few options on the market from specialist retailers, but maybe the best solution is just to drag a few cushions or a bean bag outdoors, then take it back in at the end of the day.

Containers

Many plants thrive in containers, as long as they are maintained on a regular basis. The choice of container – its shape, style or material – is important as these factors will have a definite effect on your garden. But don't be scared to think big. In a small space your containers should be incorporated into the overall plan of the garden – they should not be treated as a late addition. The distinctive style of planter could dominate a garden, so co-ordinate or contrast, but never clash.

There are plenty of options on the market, from expensive stone creations to giant mock-terracotta pots. If you want to be more avant-garde, then think about the less obvious options, such as aluminium feeding troughs and metal pipes. Galvanized metal ducting can be an interesting material for garden accessories. Although generally used for pumping steam or air through buildings, when cut into sections it can be transformed into ultra-modern containers. To complete the metamorphosis, the sections should be lined with heavy polythene or butyl liner. If you decide on a large container, it might be difficult to move when filled with soil and planted, so consider the final siting carefully.

Below: Galvanised aluminium ducting pipes have been transformed into large containers to complete a sleek hi-tech look.

Edible Eden

In the 70s self-sufficiency was all the rage. British TV sit-com *The Good Life* typified a middle-class suburban phenomenon with Mr and Mrs Average - Tom and Barbara Good - opting out of the rat race and into a life of survival on the fruits of their labour.

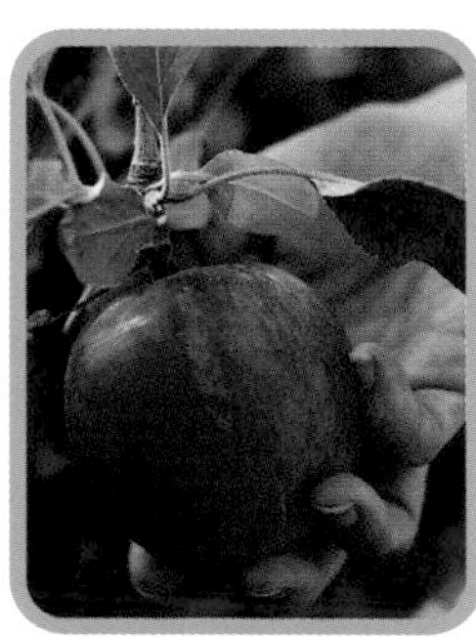

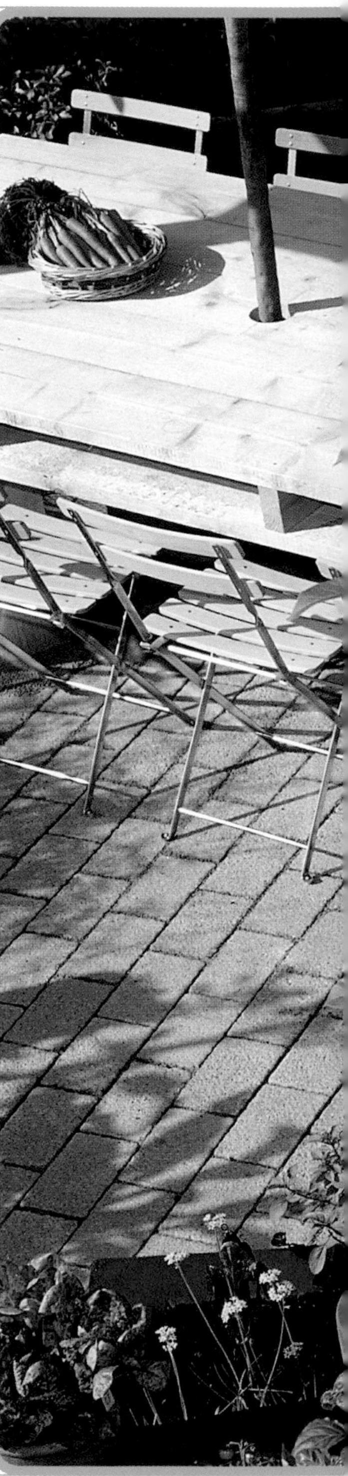

Though the Goods might seem a little extreme, the appeal of eating summer vegetables or even a few herbs from your own backyard is easily understood.

Fresh food always tastes better than the bagged or vacuum-packed sort, and cooking becomes more pleasurable when you know exactly where the ingredients have come from and what has been used to aid their cultivation. Creating an edible Eden is feasible even in a small space – whether you decide to convert your whole patio into raised beds for vegetables or simply to grow basil and parsley in your window box.

Fruit and vegetables often conjure up images of regimental rows of runner beans on allotments or dreary expanses of mud in 'dad's corner' of the garden. Today, gardening is significantly more flexible. There needn't be a harsh distinction between edible and ornamental; many edible plants are beautiful to look at. Equally, the presence of fruit and vegetables needn't rule out favourite ornamentals, as flowering plants offer the added benefit of attracting numerous insects which eat the pests that plague your edibles. This type of gardening – whether growing sunflowers from seeds or even cress on blotting paper – can also be a great way to draw children out into the garden. Section a plot off for little Johnny or Mary to introduce them to the delights of gardening and encourage an understanding of where food comes from. It beats the computer terminal any day.

paving

Despite the advent of a new range of outdoor surfaces on the market, paving is still the most popular choice for exterior floors. There are scores of options available, from traditional grey suburban slabs to ornamental cobbles. Paving is popular because it is durable, but some paving can be expensive, and all paving needs to be carefully installed to ensure it doesn't collapse or flood. Laid properly, it will need little maintenance and last, so invest in a quality material, as you could well be looking out on it for a lifetime.

Choices

Choosing the right paving isn't as simple as picking a product because you like the look of it. Practical questions have to be answered first. Is your patio aspect dark and gloomy, or sunny and bright? If it's the former, take care, as moss thrives in damp, shady conditions and can make any surface slippery. Also think of the colour: grey slabs could make it feel gloomier, whereas reddy-oranges would inject some warmth. Consider the size of your patio; a small circular patio would look fantastic constructed out of a spiral of terracotta cobbles, but this may be too expensive and time-consuming to cover a whole backyard. And finally, think of the architecture of your house and style

of your interior flooring. Victorian cobbles might look odd outside a 60s semi, and concrete slabs might seem peculiar if they butt up to French doors leading from the wooden floorboards of your living-room.

Opposite: Paving bricks create a pathway leading into an enclosed circular patio.

Pavers encompass a wide variety of styles. Concrete slabs are the most common and are quite often thrown down in rows, without much thought, outside newly-built houses. These slabs are cheap – if cost is an issue, there are ways of customizing their layout and making them more interesting. You could, for example, leave out the odd slab and plant up with herbs or chamomile for a softer look, or fill with gravel for chequer-board variation. Another highly effective look can be achieved by planting an equal margin of turf around every slab, creating a lovely mix of hard and soft surfaces.

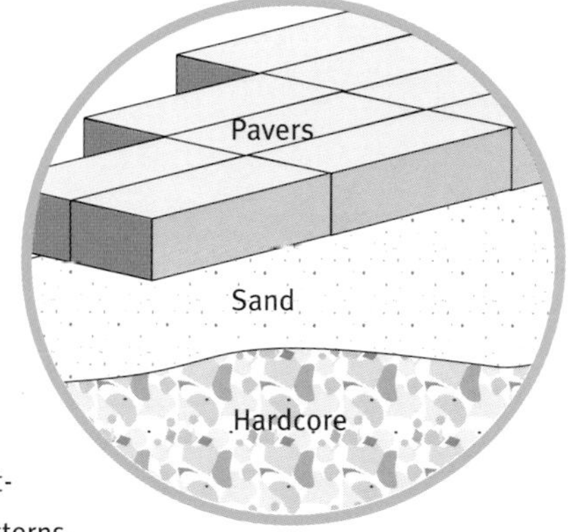

Cobbles can be bought in all different shapes and in a variety of colours. They are perfect for smaller areas and paths where you want to build up a detailed pattern. Cobbles are designed to lie directly onto a level, compressed sandbed; the cracks between blocks should be filled with sand and levelled off with a vibrating plate or whacker.

Brick is a traditional favourite for patio paving and has become a landscape classic, it blends in with almost any garden design and many types of architecture. Its basic rectangular shape enables it to be laid into different patterns, from the basic grid design to intricate woven, herringbone and circular patterns. Bricks come in a variety of colours, from the classic brick red to orangey and sandy hues. Reclaimed brick is becoming increasingly popular for the instant rustic look it can create, typical of Jekyll and Lutyens Arts and Crafts gardens. But reclaimed bricks can be more expensive than new ones and they may also be covered with old mortar, which has to be removed before laying. This can be time-consuming and, though worth persevering with, if it all seems too much bother, you can also buy new bricks which have an old and distressed look. Brick does have one disadvantage, in that many types do not withstand severe frost and will erode under heavy foot traffic. You may find that over time that you'll have to replace the occasional one.

Types of paving

Brick paving

Slabs with gravel

Cobbles

Concrete

Natural stone is the final word in sophistication, elegance and beauty. Unsurprisingly, it is the most expensive choice of flooring. Britain has a wonderful mixture of natural stones, from the dark, uncompromising set of granite, to the more gentle hue of Portland stone. Using a stone that is regional to where you live is usually successful, as it will share the same hues as not only the surrounding architecture, but quite often the soil itself. If you live in an area prone to severe winters, avoid limestone and sandstone, as they absorb water which can freeze and cause the stone to crack. Stone can be rugged or smooth – you can buy it straight from the quarry, complete with its fresh look. Reclaimed stone, by contrast, can look wonderfully worn, which always works well outdoors, instantly creating an established feel to the garden. Stone can be expensive and extremely heavy, so the initial investment should take into account the cost of employing a stonemason or bricklayer to lay it for you. Stone is a very effective material to use in a small space, just three or four choice slabs will make a significant statement.

Patio construction

It would be wonderful to say with confidence that it's easy to throw down a patio on a Sunday afternoon – unfortunately, this is not the case. Once you enter into the world of non-porous surfaces and foundations, there are no short cuts and no easy ways of putting down a patio. But, if you plan well, think hard and pay careful attention to your levels when the patio is going down, then, hopefully, you won't have to cope with the frustration of taking it up and starting all over again.

Drainage is important to allow water to seep through rather than build up into unsightly pools. Gravel is perfect for this, but slabbed areas are non-porous, so water must be encouraged to run away. The only way to do this is to build the patio on a slight slope, allowing the water to run off into a drain or lower flowerbed. This may seem to contravene the builder's code of checking everything with a spirit level, but the slope is actually so slight (1cm down every metre), that you certainly wouldn't notice it to look at.

Foundations are the basis for any garden construction, and it is a landscaper's truth that most of the blood, sweat and tears fall in parts of the garden that lie under the surface. Soil is a difficult material to manage: in winter it can swell with rain, and in summer it may harden and crack with the heat. So, to control these shifting sands, you have to put a solid slab of immovable material between the earth, the visible slabs and the rigorous pounding of feet above. In terms of how deep to dig, the short answer is the deeper the better. As a rule of thumb, excavate twice the depth of your paving slabs to add support for average garden traffic.

Slabs can be laid on a bed of compacted sand or, for a more stable patio, on a mortar bed. It's very easy to create a mortar bed: 4 parts sharp sand, 2 parts soft sand and

1 part cement is a pretty good recipe, but the real skill is in adding the right amount of water. The trick is to be careful not to let it get too runny; you want to ensure that it's firm enough to support the stones, but oozy enough for the slabs and mix to make full contact. You just need to play around with it, adding more water or more concrete until you get the right mix. Lay down enough mortar for about three slabs at a time to the depth of about 2.5cm (1in). Tap each slab with a rubber mallet to set it, then check with a straight edge and level to make sure you're keeping on track. After all the slabs are laid, let them set for twenty-four hours, then grout the joints with a lighter mortar of 3 parts soft sand and 1 part cement.

Above: An amphitheatre of mixed planting including fruit, vegetables, herbaceous plants, climbers and shrubs create a beautiful background to an outdoor dining room.

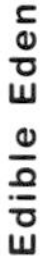

raised beds

Raised beds are the ultimate in container planting, and a wonderful space-saving planting solution for small plots. Aesthetically, they raise the height of plants, making them appear bigger and more impressive. Raised beds also surround you with plants creating a real illusion of being in a plant oasis, wherever you live. Practically, you can also fill beds with different types of soil, thus enabling plants with varying requirements to grow next to each other. Raised beds also mean fewer aches and strains, as you only have to lean into them to tend them, rather than bending over or getting down on your hands and knees all the time.

A raised bed is often the ideal solution for bringing substantial amounts of soil into small spaces and, more importantly, for containing the excess soil excavated when making decks and hard surfaces. They can also be perfect for roof terraces where everything is geared towards keeping the roof watertight. Weight, though, is an overriding factor; the raised beds will undoubtedly be the heaviest items on the terrace, and wet soil can get very heavy. If you are roof gardening, the roof must be loadbearing and the beds should be positioned over the most strongly supported part of the roof. Before constructing your bed, think carefully about where you want to position it. Do you want to grow climbers up a wall? What is the best position for maximum light? Is there plenty of room to walk around the bed and 'garden'? If you're building directly onto soil, then make sure it's level and clear of rubbish before you start. The joy of building your own raised beds is that you can construct them out of many materials, tailoring them to suit your own taste and style.

Timber is a fairly easy material to work with, and one that can be taken to pieces should you choose to change your patio design. Use tanalized timber to construct the ground-level frame to the exact size you want. Check the timber with a square to

Opposite: Raised beds around a patio will make you feel as if you are sitting in a plant oasis.

Below: Your edible Eden need not be confined just to vegetables, Ruby chard can sit happily alongside flowering plants such as Rudbeckia fulgida.

ensure it's perfectly angled, then secure it with a couple of screws. Literally build up frame by frame until you've reached the height you're after, then secure the timbers with 150x50mm (6x4in) wood posts in each corner. Leave the posts about 20cm (8in) taller than the height of your bed, so that when you turn the construction upside-down, the posts can be bedded into concrete footings as feet. Once the construction is in place, either apply a few coats of paint, or a couple of coats of wood preservative.

Railway sleepers are another good building material, as they can be stacked up, overlapping like bricks in a wall, to form a wall then lined internally with polythene and filled with soil. If you are building a particularly tall bed, then it's advisable to drill holes through the corners and insert steel rods right down into the ground for extra stability. Because railway sleepers are made from a reclaimed material, they will appear to have been in the garden for years, while still adding an element of industrial modernity.

Pressure-treated marine plywood is an excellent material for constructing lightweight beds. It's more expensive than standard timber sheeting, but, as a maritime material, it is designed to resist wind and rain. You will need to include a base for your container, as well as sides, in order to keep a rigid shape. The base should have plenty of drainage holes drilled into it, and, as with all timber constructions, the bed should be lined with heavy-duty polythene or butyl liner, perforated along the bottom. A coat of black or dark blue paint will finish it off, but, for a hi-tech finish, add an outer sleeve of aluminium or galvanized steel.

Reclaimed brick fits perfectly into cottage-style gardens, whereas cement-rendered breeze blocks and a splash of paint have a more sleek, contemporary look. They are constructed in exactly the same way as building walls, though if you want a more unusual or curved structure, it is advisable to get in a professional. It's a good idea to paint the inside of your beds with a bituminous sealer to stop water seeping out, but remember to drill some drainage holes too.

The soil mix

Filling your container isn't as simple as just chucking in a load of topsoil – drainage is absolutely paramount. Cover the container with a water-permeable, woven plastic membrane, then throw on a few handfuls of sand, before adding a lightweight soil mix to a depth of at least 45cm (18in). If weight is a consideration, as on a raised deck or roof terrace, then mix in a layer of broken polystyrene before adding the soil. Every autumn – at least for the first few years – you'll need to top it up with fresh soil as the bed settles and organic matter works its way down to the bottom.

Opposite: A tiled water rill brings a refreshing vibrancy to a circular patio.

Above: Strawberries can be plucked and brought directly the table.

Left: A selection of tomatoes ready to eat drip down from the raised beds.

edibles

You may have heard the term 'companion planting' bandied around. It's something that can cause ferocious arguments. In pure terms, it describes neighbourly plants that benefit each other by keeping away predatory insects. In softer terms, it means that vegetables, fruits, flowers and herbs work alongside insects to achieve a sustainable ecosystem that looks as good as it tastes.

Many edible plants look so beautiful you need no justification for planting them in borders. The best approach is to treat your border or bed in the same way that you would if planting herbaceous perennials. *Laurus nobilis,* or the bay tree, is quite an expensive, but worthwhile, investment. By clipping it into a strong shape, it can provide architectural interest and a pivot to all your other planting. Similarly, rows of beans and peas can add height to your border; French beans can be grown in dwarf varieties, with some bearing purple pods, whereas runner beans have wonderful reddy-orange flowers, both as good-looking as any flowering climber. Fennel is more exotic, especially the bronze varieties, which make a real splash. For height, try artichoke – it can grow up to 1.5 metres tall with wonderful silver foliage and exotic flowers.

For the rest of the border, just about anything goes. Cabbages and kale started making a comeback some years ago at fashionable events, such as the Chelsea Flower Show, and there are dozens of varieties which are perfect for small patios. Ruby chard is a stunning addition, with its vivid red stems and deep green leaves. For edible flow-

ering interest, nasturtiums and marigolds are sacrificial plants with bright flowers which attract insects from other plants. Planted around fruit trees, nasturtiums attract black fly, whereas marigolds attract hoover flies whose grubs eat aphids.

Salads in pots

For those with no patio at all, it's still possible to grow your own edibles from a window sill or in a few pots on the back step. Lettuce is incredibly easy to grow – in the spring, sprinkle a few seeds into a 20cm pot filled with compost, and six weeks later you'll have a pot brimming with salad. Choose good-looking varieties, such as Lollo Biondo and Lollo Rossa, and go for a mix of greens and purples.

Opposite left: Herbs in pots stand out from the massed planting.

Opposite right: Ruby chard brings colour and excitement when planted amongst less colourful edibles.

Left: Pots planted with a variety of salad stand in the raised walls.

In the shade of vines

A true dream for urban dwellers is often one that combines myths from ancient Rome and images of Provence – dining under the shade of a vine dripping with fruit. This is achievable with a bit of care and attention. The secret is to establish a heavy framework first of all, to take the weight of the plant as it develops. This need not be wooden trellis – a more contemporary look can be achieved by using steel RSJs, supported on a lattice of stainless steel wires that creates the 'roof'.

Below and opposite: You don' t need acres of space to grow your own grapes or apples, they will happily grow on a patio with a little care and attention.

Many grapes can do extremely well outside in this country. 'Black Hamburg' is a good variety for growing outdoors in a sunny position, it has large berries which are soft and fleshy with a fantastic flavour. A vine is a heavy feeder and drinker, so take care to prepare your soil extremely well. In mid-summer you should undertake the laborious task of thinning out individual grapes from the bunches of fruit, to allow room for proper development and to prevent fungal diseases. The shade provided by such a structure is the most natural you can achieve in a garden and, indeed, the experience is enhanced by dappled sunlight falling through the leaves and, of course, a bottle of wine.

fruit trees

The idea of reclining in a deck chair, dozing in semi-shade and reaching up to pluck an apple from a burgeoning tree, conjures up an idyllic picture. The thought of doing this on a tower block balcony or in a cramped backyard seems to be just a romantic, but unrealistic, dream. However, as city gardeners have discovered over time, nothing is impossible, so finding enough room on your patio for just one small tree is definitely worth the effort. There are plenty of different varieties of fruit tree available, so you can easily choose the perfect tree for even the smallest space.

Containers and beds

Growing fruit in containers opens up endless possibilities. More delicate fruits, such as lemon and lime, can be brought indoors during the winter months to avoid the frosts, while younger, more hardy, specimens can be kept under cover until they acclimatize.

Minarette varieties of fruiting trees make excellent container plants. Minarettes are small, trained trees which are grown on a dwarf root stock, and a more vigorous type of fruit tree is then grafted on top to create miniature fruiting trees. These will only grow between 1.8 and 2.4 metres (6-8ft) tall and so can be planted up to 60cm (2ft) apart. To ensure that the fruiting occurs right next to the main stem, trim the spurs off after the tree has fruited. The beauty of these trees is that you can grow several varieties close together in a relatively small space.

Walls

Espalier fruit trees are varieties that are trained and pruned so that their branches spur out horizontally and intertwine with each other, creating a twisted hedge arrangement. Horizontal wires attached to the wall, about 30cm (1ft) apart, are enough to get these trees started. Most fruits will do well on a sunny wall, especially soft fruit, such as peaches, plums and apricots. Shady walls are more difficult to cover, although a Morello cherry tree should be all right.

Planting and maintenance

Container fruit trees can be planted at any time, but bare-rooted fruit trees should be planted in winter. Dig a hole big enough for the roots to spread, then cover the bottom with compost and some form of enriched feed. Position the tree in the hole, then slowly sprinkle the soil back in to ensure it settles right around the roots. Water well and support with a short stake.

Fruit trees require a bit more care than the average tree or shrub – new varieties, on the other hand, require less work but will reward a little extra care and attention. Pruning is essential maintenance, not least to prevent your tree blocking out too much light from the rest of your patio. There are several approaches to this task:

- Cut branches that point inwards – to create a goblet shape.
- Festoon your tree by bending branches down when the tree is young, and attaching them to the trunk with wire.
- Cut back all current growth to a few buds, then prune again in winter, for a tree covered with spurs.

Opposite: An apple tree grafted onto a dwarf root stock produces fruit on short spurs. This tree is perfectly at home in a raised bed surrounded by ornamental planting.

Guide to dwarf root stock

PIXIE:. Smallest dwarf for small containers
M27: Very dwarf – ideal for containers or small raised beds.
MM106:Medium sized – suitable for small growing spaces.
M26: Semi-dwarf.
M9: Dwarf, but needs a stake for support.

extras

Outdoor eating

Food tastes great al fresco, and however small our plots, we invariably try to squeeze in the smallest table and chairs. But when siting your dining area, take these considerations into account:

- Make sure there is good access from the house – carrying plates of food and glasses can become precarious if you're negotiating large shrubs or ponds along the way.
- Think realistically about how many people you want to seat at once. There's no sense in filling the whole patio with a table for ten when ninety per cent of the time it'll just be you and your partner eating outdoors.
- Allow for shade – eating outside can become very uncomfortable if the sun is beating down on you throughout the whole meal. Shade can be provided by large umbrellas, customised canopies, curtains or even a plant-covered pergola.
- Think about the evening sun – few of us are able to enjoy our gardens all day long, so catching the last evening rays over dinner and a glass of wine can feel like paradise.

Left: For many people the patio is an area for dining and entertaining and a place for relaxing day or night.

- Choose appropriate furniture – designer models are fine if you have somewhere to store them; if not, opt for year-round wooden or iron models.
- Don't surround your eating area with too much fragrant planting. If it smells attractive to you, it will inevitably hold the same attraction for insects and bees – who may be friends to the flowers, but are not our ideal dinner date.

Edible flowers

Edible flowers come in a variety of shapes, colours and flavours. The most commonly-used are nasturtiums, carnations, marigolds, violets and snapdragons. Always remember to check from more than one reliable source that your flower is edible, and that it has been grown organically.

DIY composts

An easy and eco-friendly way to produce your own compost is with a worm bin. Worms will turn almost all kitchen waste, whether potato peelings or tea bags, into superb compost. Worms are a gardener's best friend, breaking down organic matter and spreading it through the soil. Another advantage of wormeries is that they are more compact than regular compost bins and can be squeezed into very small spaces.

Japan

The Japanese garden is the little black dress of the garden world – a classic that is always in fashion. In recent years it has become intensely popular throughout the western world, as it offers so many solutions to contemporary interests and modern living.

A Japanese-style garden radiates peace and tranquillity, providing a contemplative space away from our hectic, fast-paced world. However, to the uninitiated it might appear to be merely a low-maintenance, pretty garden. But this would be to misinterpret its simplicity. The key to successfully creating a Japanese patio is a basic understanding of the principles from which such gardens originate, combined with a practical approach to modern-day, western living.

In a traditional Japanese garden, natural materials, such as stone and wood, combine with predominantly green plants to form the basis of a landscape that is a study of oriental principles, philosophy and religion. The carefully selected planting is continually pruned and clipped, while the placing of stone, gravel or ornamentation has hugely symbolic meaning and representation.

Though we might not grasp the deeper symbolism, it might be that this type of garden is perfect for small, enclosed plots or courtyards. When planned and executed with care and attention to detail, a Japanese garden can create a harmonious, relaxing space. So rather than trying to emulate a true Japanese garden, it's probably better to recreate its most appealing elements simply as a pleasing and attractive picture. We are becoming increasingly aware of the beauty of natural materials and many interior spaces in recent years have included displays of pebbles, cobbles and sea shells. Of course, outdoors is the perfect home for such materials which, when set alongside plants, can create a wonderful, serene garden.

flooring

One of the real secrets of a Japanese garden is that from the beginning it doesn't look new. This typically timeless quality can be achieved in the fabric of the garden by careful consideration of the material used. For hard landscaping it's best to use a reclaimed material, whether wood or stone. Recycling natural resources is not only eco-friendly, but also helps create that timeless quality. An old piece of wood, for example, contains inherent beauty and character. Stone fresh from a quarry, by contrast, will often seem bright and brash and may need time to 'mature'.

Looking for reclaimed materials can be great fun giving us a chance to get away from the uniform conditions, sizes and finishes that garden centres and DIY stores offer. Sources of reclaimed materials can be architectural yards, farms, or buildings being demolished, either advertised in the yellow pages or the small ads. Ironically

it's fashionable to distress many new materials to make them appear old. But be careful and scrupulous about who and where you buy from.

Railway sleeper decking

Among the most obvious reclaimed materials suitable for use outdoors are old railway sleepers. Beautiful hunks of wood generally of uniform size, they have already served a purpose in the transportation of goods and people throughout the country. They're made for outdoor life and for traffic. Until relatively recently, we've been more used to seeing them employed in the garden as raised beds and steps (see page 74). But they make a great decking material.

There are some pitfalls, though. Railway sleepers are extremely heavy, so always have at least two strong people on hand to carry them. Manoeuvring them into position in a back garden without a side access can be a nightmare. When buying, take care either to buy from a reputable dealer or choose them in person, as the quality of material can vary. A common problem can be the secretion of tar on a hot day or indeed a constant fresh smell of creosote that may take some time to disperse. It's also important not to use sleepers that are cracked and rotten – well past their sell-by date. Another difficulty with sleepers is that they are extremely hard to cut, so you may need to enlist the help of a trained chainsaw user if you want to create elaborate shapes. Despite the problems, though, sleepers do create a beautiful effect and are well worth the time, effort and financial investment. Remember too that wooden decks should be constructed only in open, sunny positions.

Installation of railway sleeper deck

Because of their striking visual qualities, railway sleeper decks are often slightly elevated off the ground. This not only shows up their beautiful surface appearance, but also lets you see the edge and depth of the wood. If raised about 2–3cm (around 1in) above terra firma, a slight shadow can be created all around the decks, almost giving the appearance that they are floating (see 'Sea view', p104). Or, as a contrast, two areas of interlinking deck can be created: one sunk to ground level and one slightly raised.

Before going shopping, carefully measure your site and calculate the amount of wood you will need. Railway sleepers will often be 2.5–2.8m (9–9ft) in length, 20cm (9in) wide and 15cm (6in) deep. Decide on the shape of your overall patio. For a small area, it may be possible to create a square-shaped patio using about ten sleepers laid side by side, with no cutting involved. This is a quick, dramatic and easy solution. Curved shapes are, of course, more complex. The weight of the sleeper will usually be enough to keep it in place without mortar. A base of hard core 3cm (about 1in) deep should be constructed and levelled off and the sleepers laid on top.

Opposite: Japanese gardens tend to have a timeless quality, which is reflected here through the use of natural materials, including wooden decking, gravel, boulders and cut stone slabs.

Above: A circular patio made from reclaimed railway sleepers is a beautiful final focal point in the garden.

Gravel

A wonderful, easy and cheap material to use in a garden, gravel can provide a great link between different elements and a fantastic mulch around the base of plants. However, because of the current fad for gravel gardening, we are in danger of overusing this resource. It's a fluid material that works well in contemporary or traditional settings but finds its true home in a Japanese garden. Gravel as a flooring material has become trendy because it's low-maintenance. In a true Japanese garden, gravel or granite sand may be carefully raked into swirls by Buddhist monks. It may represent lakes or seas and is to be viewed from a distance and not walked on.

A huge variety of colours is available, so it can be very easy to link in with an existing colour scheme or to brighten and enhance a shady area. Gravel has become a

favourite material for driveways and pathways. Prepare the ground well by digging up all weeds, making sure to clear out perennial roots. A 7cm (2½ in) base of hard core should be laid and compacted. Bricks set on edge or strips of marine plywood can be used to contain the material and to create an edging line. It's important not to choose too small a grade as particles can get wedged in the sole of your shoe and cause an annoyance or even be walked into the house.

Natural stone

Of all the options for garden paving, natural stone is by far the most beautiful and luxurious, which means it can be the most expensive, too. It can require a great deal of expertise to prepare your site for paving, to cut and lay the stone (see p70). Throughout the country, and indeed the world, different types of stone with varying characteristics are available. The most common and among the easiest to use is sandstone, but granite, limestone, slate and marble are also popular. Each of these selections will have their own strong characteristics. Some, such as marble, will be harder than others, while often the colour, such as a dark slate, will be quite strong. Reclaimed second-hand flagstones are generally sold by the metre, but in recent years have become as expensive as, or even more expensive than, newly quarried stone. If you are choosing stone from a reclamation yard, try and stick with one main type to prevent your garden looking like a 70s crazy paving nightmare. Stone slabs randomly set with gravel, turf or alpine planting in between can create a very acceptable patio.

Opposite: A shallow rill with running water divides a pebble pathway and leads into a circular pond.

Below left: Cobbles of various sizes sourced from an inland quarry contrast beautifully with the foliage of a Japanese maple.

Below right: New cut stone slabs create a pathway through the cobbled garden.

water

Water can be both an exciting and relaxing addition to any garden but this is especially so in the Japanese garden, where water is revered as a main life force of the natural world. Whether used for its still reflective qualities, mirroring plants and foliage, or to be enjoyed for its flowing refreshing glint, water introduces light and life into even the smallest space.

Rills

A rill is a channel of running water, much like a miniature canal. In a garden, the rill will be located at a set distance from the source of the host water – a pond or basin. This reservoir of water need not necessarily be seen – it could be held in underground tanks. The main priority of the reservoir is that it holds enough water to feed the rill and keep a submersible pump in operation. The pump circulates the water from the reservoir in a pipe hidden either just below ground level or overground, disguised by foliage. The pipe re-emerges at the mouth of the rill, gushing water which then flows through an often decorative waterway, drawn back to the reservoir by gravity.

Opposite: Geranium *'Johnson's Blue' creates an edging in a slightly shady corner next to the water rill.*

Left: Cobbles are an attractive material for lining ponds as water has a wonderful effect on them, enhancing their natural colours.

There are countless materials from which a rill can be constructed, including overlapping strips of butyl liner, concrete, steel girders and marine plywood, which can then be tiled in mosaic. Another option is to make both the bowl-shaped pool and the linking rills by creating a base of concrete, which you then coat with mortar and set with cobblestones.

Cobbles are small rounded stones that have been water-worn in river beds or in the sea. They are best taken from inland quarries where removing them won't harm the environment. Most cobbles are egg-shaped and come in a variety of colours. They work particularly well with water, either when used as natural edging round a pool or when carefully crafted into a channel over which water can run. Sparkling water has a wonderful effect on stone, setting all their colours alight.

Constructing a cobbled pond

Laying natural cobbles is a laborious task, so allow plenty of time. It's a true craft, which initially will seem like a nightmare. It's best to pack the cobbles very closely together – they often work well on their side. Lay a base of hardcore a little below the required depth of the pond, cover it with fresh mortar, then set the cobbles into it. It's best to set the cobbles in the same direction.

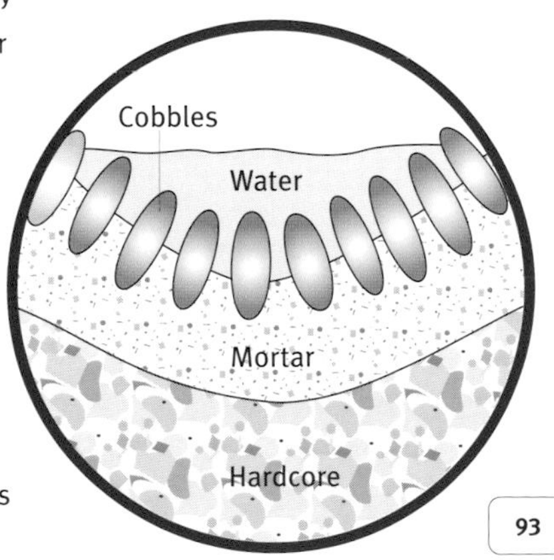

When creating a cobbled rill and pool as a feature in a garden, plant as close as possible to the edge of the water to soften the hard effect. Let the rill occasionally disappear under the arching branches of a Japanese maple. Complete the picture by placing occasional loose, large boulders at the water's edge as sculptural features.

Ponds and pools

Even on the smallest patio you can have water – it needn't be a complicated process. Water does different things for different people; a shallow bird-bath can create a charming focal point and a fascinating spectacle; or a fountain or plain gushing gurgle

of water can dance up and drench boulders before disappearing into a hidden, and therefore safe, reservoir. Of course, this sort of water feature will need a submersible pump and as a result your entertainment will be available on demand at the flick of a switch.

If you don't have enough space to incorporate a rill and/or a pond, but would like a water feature in keeping with the uncomplicated Japanese minimalist style, you could make a pond from a wooden half-barrel filled with water. Wooden barrels are easily available from your garden centre and shouldn't need lining providing it is well-made. To complement the natural effect of the barrel, set the pond on paving stones or gravel, with simple, delicate planting either in or around it.

Opposite: A circular pool in the small courtyard garden reflects the sky above in a confined space.

Left and above: Even the smallest garden can have a water feature; here an oak half-barrel is planted with aquatics.

japanese planting

Japanese gardening uses plants in a symbolic way – giving the garden deep emotional, intellectual and spiritual dimensions. The overall picture presented is of a green sculpted landscape, perfect in every way, with occasional springtime bursts of colour from azaleas and cherry trees. Plants are chosen for their dramatic sculptural quality, as well as how they will relate to the natural materials in the garden.

Japanese gardens are designed to be complete and fully-grown from the outset, and to present the same scene over many years. The essence of the Japanese garden is to create an atmosphere that is tranquil and peaceful, achieved by a minimalist design and by choosing native trees and shrubs that are in harmony with the surrounding countryside.

Many familiar suburban plants in Britain originated in Japan and our relatively temperate climate is the key to their success. The Japanese garden has a definite balance of colour all year round, with structural plants, such as the pine and the bamboo, retaining a steady presence after the maples have lost their showy autumnal leaves. Subtle variations in leaf and bark colour and texture are highly valued.

Bamboo is revered in Japan, as it is associated with the moon, is long-lived, and often evergreen. Bamboo is the ideal big plant for a small space, as it acts as a screen without blocking out the available light. It also sounds great when the wind rustles through it.

Pine symbolizes longevity. It's a big group, ranging from small ground-cover trees that are almost shrub-like to massive forest specimens. Other plants that are also closely associated with Japanese gardens include *pieris*, rhododendrons, camellias and maples.

Japanese maple is an essential plant in an oriental garden. It prefers a sheltered spot, as rough winds can burn its delicately cut leaves. There are many varieties of maple to choose from, but all will delight with a blaze of crimson and orange shades in the autumn. A maple is a perfect specimen tree for a small courtyard area and can also be ideal for large containers.

If your garden is in the country and has the benefit of an unpolluted atmosphere, moss can be encouraged to act as the main ground cover. In inner city areas moss could be substituted with *Pachysandra terminalis* or *epimediums*.

A good western substitute for a Japanese plant is *Euonymus alatus*, the spindle bush. Its leaves curl and hang from branches, turning a blood red in the autumn.

Far left: Cercidiphyllum japonicum *is a deciduous Japanese tree. Its leaves provide a wonderful spectacle in the autumn, turning from their youthful bronze to yellow, then orange and red in the autumn.*

Centre and left: Plants such as the acer palmatum atropurpureum *give an authentic feel to a Japanese garden, even when surrounded by more traditional English planting.*

extras

Often in a Japanese garden what might look like a carefully placed group of stones in fact represents a mountain range. Similarly, statuary, especially figures of the Buddha, are revered sacred symbols. A tea house or pavilion is much more than somewhere to stop off for a cuppa; the tea ceremony in Japanese society is based on religious and spiritual traditions that emphasize taking time out from frenetic activity.

Granite lanterns and water bowls have a refined history. Although it's interesting to learn a little about them, we should understand that their use in our pastiche Japanese garden is essentially decorative. Many of these features are beautifully made from wood or stone and their design is pleasing to the eye – they compare favourably with gaudy European and American garden paraphernalia such as white plastic swans, Victorian lamps and multi-coloured gnomes fishing in ponds. While peace and tranquillity can be suggested by granite bowls of water, curiosity is stimulated by the steady wooden knock of a deer scarer, and excitement and entertainment by an arched red bridge in the distance. But the Buddha of Suburbia still remains an icon of ornamentation rather than a serene and meaningful experience, unless you're a Buddhist!

To complete the sino-Japanese look, why not clad your fences in instant roll-out bamboo, and float wax candles among your water lilies. A pair of wooden sandals left on the bank of the stream could even suggest a bathing geisha. And, of course, no picnic is complete without the obligatory willow-patterned china and chopsticks.

Opposite: The final picture of a Japanese garden is created by the addition of a stone lantern and granite basin, which are not only ornamental, but also signify religious rituals.

Using objects as focal points.

Careful consideration must be given to the placement of any objets d'art in the garden. As you journey through the plot, these features should enhance the design of your garden, aid contemplation, or just be viewed for their beauty and aesthetic appeal. These objects represent man and the garden.

Placing objects, such as stone basins, lanterns or buddhas, can be extremely difficult in a brand new garden, as they work best against established foliage. There should be a sense of mystery, of surprise – they should not all be visible from one view, and they should send out individual messages as you come across each one. You could place a stone basin on your way to the teahouse to suggest that you purify yourself with water; or a Buddha could be the subtle focal point of the final view, set in a peaceful position where meditation seems appropriate; or a lantern could illuminate a path or be placed at the edge of water where the flame is reflected, adding mystery.

Use these objects as the punctuation marks of your garden design – the exclamation marks or full stops – but don't let them dominate, or their effect is paradoxically lessened. In most gardens, to even attempt to adhere to formal Zen traditions amounts to no less than parody, so follow the basic design rules and place objects where they please you.

Sea view

The ever-changing light, cloud formations, colour and drama of a seascape create a picture that can be hard to capture in a design for the average patio plot. But for many people a country garden or one with a sea-view is a fantasy they long to realize, even if only in part, to provide the ultimate escape, just short of their own desert island.

Over the years, show gardens at Chelsea and Hampton Court have tried to perfect the idea of a seaside garden. But the effect has been to parody it.

In the same way, planning a patio or a garden in a coastal situation offers breathtaking adventures but also involves severe limitations. Abandon any thoughts of creating or maintaining a traditional or organized garden. Different rules apply on almost every level. In some senses to create a man-made garden in an area of outstanding beauty is an anomaly. Nothing we hope to create will ever compete with the natural scene that originally inspired us.

Before human beings existed there were many species of plants and animals. In a natural, non-contrived environment that

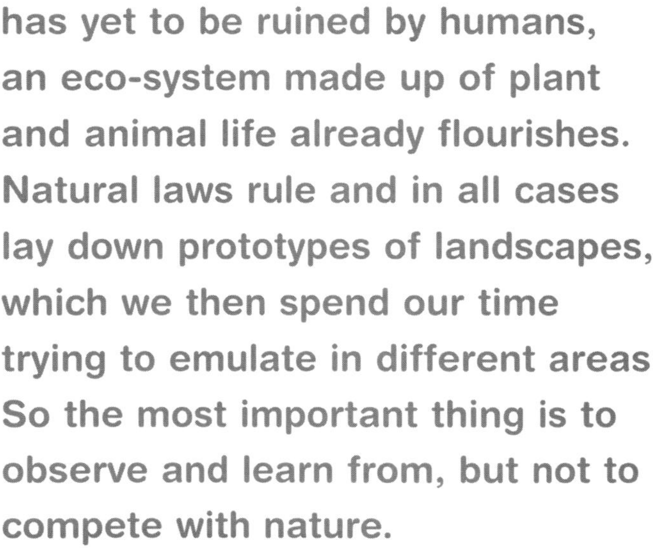

has yet to be ruined by humans, an eco-system made up of plant and animal life already flourishes. Natural laws rule and in all cases lay down prototypes of landscapes, which we then spend our time trying to emulate in different areas. So the most important thing is to observe and learn from, but not to compete with nature.

Your view or, in gardening terms, your backdrop is so overwhelming that you mustn't try to compete with it. The eye of the gardener and visitor alike will always be drawn to the furthest point on the horizon and everything you plan for your plot will only ever play a supporting role.

The conditions that such a scene provides will always be the dominant issue for a gardener. On a calm, sunny day everything will appear rosy and heavenly but, as any sailor will tell you, things can change in an instant. The battle that nature wages involves strong salt-laden winds and exposed conditions. Species that tolerate these situations have evolved over the millennia. The gardener's desire often conflicts with nature – our aim being to grow as many different types of plants in one plot. It's a conflict that can be played either as a farce or for fun. However, it will always be a drama.

raised patios

Wherever there are thoughts of escape and castaways, wooden rafts come into play. A raft in a garden can be a simple wooden construction created like a deck and used as an elevated viewing platform. Its beauty and magic lie in the fact that it floats above the garden, allowing a sea of plants – be they wild grasses or cultivated species – to grow around its base and even peep through openings and cracks. A raised raft can act as a real escape – it can be a focal point, an object of beauty in itself or a practical resource which, when mounted, will give an optimum view of the seascape. A raft is especially exciting for children, as it could be easily adapted to house a flagpole with a skull and cross bones fluttering in the breeze. Or the raft could be simply a solid flooring on which a cup of tea can be enjoyed each morning while you take in the views and assess the weather of the day.

Constructing the raft is simple – set four heavy, treated timber posts into the ground and secure with concrete. Depending on your levels, construct a timber framework of beams at least 15cm (6in) from the ground. On top of this, lay your final flooring, which could be reclaimed timber, new decking wood or even railway sleepers. The wood should be left to weather, rather than be treated with any artificial colouring. The shape of the raft can be independent of any other shape in the garden, as within a relatively short period of time, planting will hide its edges. Try and keep the construction as simple as possible – the main focus is the sea.

The raised patio could be complemented by a second patio with which you could adopt a slightly more conventional approach. This one could be sited in an area that makes the most of internal views in the garden and takes advantage of whatever shelter is available – perhaps located close to the house. It could be of a similar or of a contrasting shape to the previous one and even constructed from a different material.

Opposite: Two oval-shaped patios – one made from polished concrete, the other a raised wooden deck – create usable hard surfaces in a coastal Edinburgh garden.

Left: Hard-leaved Phormium tenax *is used to withstanding the elements.*

outdoor finishes

Hard landscaping materials make up the practical surfaces in a garden – walls, patios, decks and even rockeries fall into this category. Traditionally we have used materials, such as clay bricks, natural stone, concrete slabs or timber fencing, but recently we've begun to make use of more innovative materials, ones that up to now would have seemed out of place in a garden. A prime example is concrete – the various types of rendered finish, dyes and paint available now can change and enhance any surface. Walls can be clad in a variety of metals, even in plastic and rubber, which are now being used in gardens for the first time. When considering the possibilities of what a garden can be, don't forget the wide choice of materials and what effect and finish they can have on your structures as a whole.

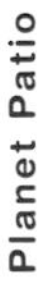

Concrete

Although concrete may not immediately appeal to the aesthetic tastebuds, it is worth exploring for the different qualities it has to offer. Among its advantages are flexibility and durability; as a fluid material it's easy to set in exciting or symmetrical shapes. It's cheap, readily available and, when polished (a monotonous, labour-intensive job), its aggregate content is ground to a flat finish, revealing a pattern that shimmers when wet.

It can seem absurd to introduce water in such an environment but a simple circular depression ground into your patio may create a shallow bathing pool for birds or simply act as a mirror to reflect the sky on the concrete surface. Leave it up to the elements to provide the water, so that nature decides when you have a water feature.

Marmarino plaster

A wonderful and fairly recent finish to be introduced to surfaces in gardens is marmarino plaster. Applying this finish is a very skilled job and should be undertaken only by an expert. Marmarino plaster is a mixture of lime and marble dust which is applied very thinly, layer after layer. It almost has the appearance of fine china, and in a coastal situation, where natural light is changing constantly, the effects can be beguiling. A hole in the wall enhances the drama of the structure, creating an awareness of the space behind, and affords the opportunity of framing a simple view to the back of your feature.

Opposite: A curved wall acts as both a sculptural and sheltering background to the oval patio.

Left: A circular window in the wall helps to complete the sculptural effect and creates a sense of mystery.

Above: A shallow puddle has been carved out of the oval patio and fills with water when it rains.

Right: A firepit is sunk into the ground to provide a warm seating area sheltered by planting.

Opposite: The firepit can, of course, double up as a barbecue on which to grill food, and as an unconventional garden dining space.

heat

When you have invested time and resources into creating a garden that's a joy to be in, especially one with spectacular views, it is a shame to have to abandon it because of the cold or simply because of the dark. Heat and light are something that we've recently begun to appreciate outdoors, although in a rural situation both can seem oddly suburban when provided through modern means. By contrast, a natural bonfire is a luxury we can all enjoy and basic food can be easily grilled over open flames.

There are no hard and fast rules about creating an open fire in a garden – it may be that a few simple boulders set in a ring will protect developing flames. But it's not a good idea to light fires in built-up areas – you need to consider your neighbours and some local authorities will have very definite rules on when and where fires are allowed. Never plan a fire in open countryside among any dry vegetation or in the shade of overhanging trees, and in your garden, make sure no shrubs are in danger from heat damage.

Firepit

If your site is very windy or exposed it may be an idea to build a firepit below ground level. This can be done by excavating 50cm (20in) of soil and building up two rings of bricks – a central one 30cm (1ft) wide and an outer one of 1–1.2m (3–4ft). When lined with brick, the outer ring of soil can provide recessed seating and the inner one can house your flames. A simple grill resting above the flames will be all you need to cook al fresco. Using this system is certainly a change from the traditional barbecue or outdoor heater, but it also demands extra care and attention for safe use, so it's not the best choice if there are children around. But the flickering light of naked flames in a garden helps to create an air of mystery and romance.

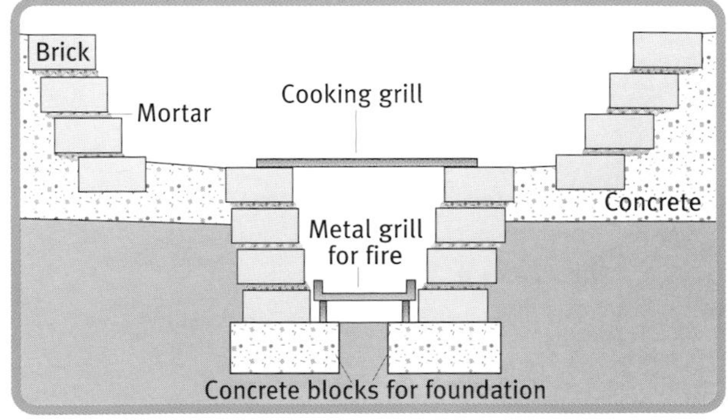

planting

Coastal gardens are at the mercy of the sea and wind. Constant battering by wind will dry out plants and, at worst, uproot them. To add to this the winds on the coast carry salt, which scorches plants. The combination of fierce gales carrying salt can be devastating – from literally shredding leaves on trees to deforming and blackening foliage. There is an almost perpetual battle being waged between the elements, on the one hand, and plants on the other.

Therefore, to have any chance of success, your garden needs some shelter. You can create a manmade barrier, or plant a natural windbreak. The best form of shelters filter the wind – wattle fencing, trees and shrubs. Solid walls tend to cause more turbulence. But while you do want to keep out the wind, you don't want to block the wonderful view, so bear this in mind when establishing a shelter.

Once the protection is established it is possible to grow a wide range of ornamental trees and shrubs. For best results, stick to those that are known to flourish in coastal conditions. Walk around the locality and see what's thriving in other gardens. The same plants will appear again and again. As part of their evolution, plants native to coastal regions have developed inbuilt protection. Grey-foliaged plants, such as lavender and *Senecio*, do well by the sea, as the surface of their leaves are covered with minute hairs. The salt can only reach the tips of the hairs, so rain washes away the salt crystals. Plants with high-glossed leaves, such as *Elaeagnus,* are a good choice, as the waxy covering acts as a film that protects the leaves from absorbing the salt crystals. Some leaves have developed especially tough skins, for example *Hebe*. And other shrubs exude a sticky gum on the leaf surface, for example *Escallonia*. Once you bear these rules in mind, you will begin to develop your own idea of what plants might be suitable for your conditions.

Right: Hebe *and* Pinus *(opposite) both possess leaves with hard cuticles which will withstand salt-laden winds and are perfect for coastal situations.*

Suitable choices may include:

Pinus radiata trees (Monterey pine) and *Quercus ilex* (evergreen oak) form good windbreaks by the sea.

Olearia (daisy bush) is a great choice, offering masses of white daisy flowers in the summer and interesting holly-like foliage.

Phormium tenax (New Zealand flax) is commonly seen around the coast and seems happy with any amount of punishment. It's a spiky, architectural plant that provides interesting form and all-year colour.

Lavatera and *buddleia* are fast growing and will protect slower-growing plants. They also flower profusely.

Hippophae rhamnoides (sea buckthorn) is a thorny shrub which makes a great windbreak. It's very tough but also much underrated in the looks department – with attractive silver needle leaves that protect themselves from salt spray. You need to grow male and female plants to get the beautiful orange berries in the autumn.

Escallonia rubra var. macrantha is a vigorous evergreen shrub that makes an attractive seaside hedge, producing an abundance of small red flowers. Its leathery leaves are well able to withstand salt spray.

Lavandula (lavender) is an old favourite which is perfectly happy by the sea. This

From left to right: Olearia, Potentilla, Lavatera *and* Phormium *are plants which provide different types of interest in a coastal garden, whether it is leaf shape, flowers or composition.*

evergreen shrub is bushy, with dense spikes of fragrant purple flowers and narrow, aromatic, silvery-grey leaves.

Arbutus unedo (strawberry tree) is so-called for the fruits it produces in the autumn, which strongly resemble strawberries, though in appearance rather than in taste. Other points of interest include its beautiful orange brown bark, white urn-shaped flowers in autumn and evergreen glossy leaves.

Kniphofia (red hot poker) has spikes of orange flowers which appear in late autumn and add drama and colour to a coastal garden.

Hebe species is suitable for seaside gardens and many bear attractive flowers.

Planting tips

- **Although you may be tempted to use large plants for instant impact, smaller plants are better able to adapt to their environment.**
- **In very exposed areas, consider using a windbreak of plastic or wattle for the first two years to help plants establish. This will lessen the amount of turbulence, in effect creating a type of microclimate around the plants.**
- **Plant in spring to help plants establish quickly.**
- **Often in coastal regions the soil is sandy and therefore extremely free draining, To help maintain moisture around the roots of the plant, add plenty of well-rotted compost or other humus material. This will absorb any moisture and act as a type of capillary mat to give the plant a drink when it needs it.**

extras

Patio with a view

If you are lucky enough to have a coastal view, you will, of course, want to get the maximum benefit from it. A raised deck is a perfect surface for seating and offers a wonderful viewing platform, whether made from scattered old packing cases – which can double-up as simple, yet stylish, chairs or tables – or from a hammock suspended across the boards.

When deciding on your furniture, and indeed on any type of patio accessory, consider whether it suits your garden as well as your sense of style – although you may long for the latest line in café society chrome furniture, a coastal garden may not be the best place for it. Remember, too, that often these accessories can be the focal point of your garden, as you look out of the window from your home, so choose things that blend in and are durable. It's nice to be able to leave these features *in situ* all year round.

Garden heaters

By their nature, coastal gardens tend to be windswept and fairly chilly, but outdoor heaters are a brilliant solution to this problem. Not only can they provide heat in really cold weather, but they are also a great addition to any patio on a cool summer evening, allowing you to make the most of your garden all year round.

Heaters come in a wide selection of shapes and sizes: some simple ones are reminiscent of single-bar electric fires, while other gas models add style to function with a flourish. Heaters are not a cheap accessory, but they will add a little touch of luxury and a comforting warmth to your al fresco dining.

Opposite: Old packing cases, used as seats or tables, blend into the wooden deck.

Left: Although a raised deck makes the most of a sea view, such an exposed situation can get cold. Outdoor heaters are wonderful additions to gardens, making them comfortable places for entertaining all year round.

and finally

Thanks to the series producer of *Planet Patio*, Andy Francis, Executive producer, Rachel Innes-Lumsden, editor, Franny Moyle, directors Ann Wilson, Paul Vanezis and Micci Billinger.

Thanks to Sara Marsh, Bina Mistry, Trupti Magecha (for making me an honorary Hindu), Julie Mason, Christine Hardman, Karen Hope, Lucyina Moodie, Caron Brown, Silvana Franco, Candida Allfrey, Richard Firth, Michelle Davies, Jason Evans, Anne Waterhouse, Colin Rowbottom, John Nichol, Louis Massie.

Special thanks to Jane Root, Julie Savill, Adam Pascoe and all at *Gardeners World* magazine, BBC *Good Homes* magazine, and beeb.com. Thanks to all at John Noel Management, especially Nik, John, Polly, Debbie and Brian.

Thanks to Joan, Jack, Declan, Niamh, Emer, David, Gerry, Ronan, Terry, Madeleine, Jane, Karl, Tim, Natasha, Julia, Holly, Ben, Yayee, Wendy O'Connalaigh, Tom Curran, Vincent Barnes, Bernard O'Rourke, Barry Cotter, Sean Keirghan, Anita Notaro, Pat Dixon, Vicky Jebb, Pat, Jane, Eilis, Rory, Niall, Renee and the Mannings in Liverpool.

Thanks to Craig Knowles and Robin Matthews for their wonderful photographs of the gardens.

Thanks to Helena Caldon for persistence and patience, to Nicky Copeland for persistence and love, to Seamus Geoghegan, Robin and Alice Wood, Lisa Pettibone and Bea Thomas.

Thanks to superman Sean Cunningham, project manager.

And to my beautiful wife Justine for all her help and support.

directory

LA STORY

Decking

International Timber
West Yard
Trafford Wharf Road
Trafford Park
Manchester M17 1DJ
Tel: 0161 848 2900
(South African Karri Hardwood)

Tri-Coated Decking Screws
Protim Solignum
Fieldhouse Lane
Marlow
Buckings SL7 1LS
Tel 01628 486644

Camron PR (Representing the Softwood Timber Decking Association)
7 Floral Street
London WC2 E9D
Tel: 020 7420 1700

Ronseal Ltd
Thorncliffe Park
Chapel Town
Sheffield S35 2YP
Tel: 0114 240 9351

Lighting

Clifton Lighting Company
Marchdyke House
Mill Hill
Brockweir
Monmouthshire NP16 7NW
Tel: 01291 689372

Building Materials

E H Smith
Head office:
1 Sherbourne Road
Acocks Green
Birmingham B27 6AB
Tel: 0121 745 4101

Buttington Quarry
Welshpool
Powys SY21 8SZ
Tel: 01938 570 375

Special Formwork Ltd
Stubbers Green Road,
Aldridge,
West Midlands WS9 8BN
Tel: 01922 451 909

Safety Wear

Spartan Safety Wear
857 Romford Road
Manor Park
London E12 5JY
Tel: 020 8514 3675

Tool Hire

Wilkinson Sword
Fiskars UK Ltd
Newlands Avenue
Bridgend
Mid Glamorgan
Tel: 01656 655595

Stanley
Drakehouse Plant
Beighton Road East
Drakehouse
Sheffield S20 7JZ
Customer Service: 08701 650650

Ralph Martindale (Birmingham Ltd)
Crocodile House
Strawberry Lane
Willenhall
West Midlands WV13 3RS
Tel: 01902 826826

Haemmerlin
The Washington Centre
Halesowen Road
Netherton
West Midlands
Tel: 01384 243243

Rapid Hire (UK) Limited
Intersection House
110 Birmingham Road
West Bromwich B70 6RX
Tel: 0121 500 0700

Van Hire

LDV Ltd
Drews Lane
Birmingham B8 2QG
Tel: 0121 322 3000

Skips

SITA
Waste Care Management
Montague Street
Birmingham B9 4BA
Tel: 0121 643 6430

Plants

The Herb Nursery
Thistleton
Oakham
Rutland LE15 7RE
Tel: 01572 767 658

Poyntzfield Herb Nursery
Black Isle
By Dingwall
Ross & Cromarty
Scotland IV7 8LX
Tel: 01381 610352

Tendercare
Southlands Road
Denham, Uxbridge
Middlesex UB9 4HD
Tel: 01895 835544

Webbs Garden Centres Ltd
Wychbold
Droitwich
Worcester WR9 0DG
Tel: 01527 861777

Arne Herbs
Limeburn Nurseries
Limeburn Hill
Chew Magna
Bristol BS40 8QW
Tel: 01275 333399

Canal Side Landscape & Garden Supplies
Rabone Lane, Smethwick
Birmingham B66 3JL
Tel: 0121 555 7180

Natural Products

Comfort & Joy
Baytree Cottage
Eastleach
Nr. Cirencester
Gloucestershire GL7 3NL
Tel: 01367 850278

Terracotta Pots

Classic Pot Emporium
30A Straight Road
Boxford, Colchester
Essex Co4 5HN
Tel: 01206 271 946

Apta Pottery
Dencora Way
Leacon Road
Fairwood Business Park
Ashford
Kent TN23 4FH
Tel: 01233 621090
www.sales@apta.co.uk
(Will provide details of local stockist in your area)

Loungers

Banana Lounger
(bright pink plastic lounger)
Mail order from Cubic
Tel: 020 8671 5737
www.cubicuk.com
Also available from a range of stockists, call above number for details.

Lido Lounger
Furniture On Line
www.furniture-on-line.co.uk
Tel: 0113 2436500

Zeta Lounger
Indian Ocean Online Store
www.Indian-Ocean.co.uk
Tel: 020 8675 4808

Bikini Lounger
Available from: Chart Interiors
Tel: 01342 326659

Silver ball, Lido, Phantom, O sole mio
The Modern Garden Company
P O Box 5868
Dunmow CM6 2FB
Tel: 01279 851 900
email:info@moderngarden.co.uk
www.moderngarden.co.uk

Constantian Recliner
Gardens and Beyond
1265 High Road
Whetstone
London N20 9HS
Tel: 020 8445 6446
www.gardensbeyond.com

'Chaise' Lounger
by Theo Williams
Space
214 Westbourne Grove
London W11
Tel: 020 7229 6533
Tel: 020 8472 0521

VIVA AL FRESCO

Skips
SITA
Waste Care Management
Montague Street
Birmingham B9 4BA
Tel: 0121 643 6430
Tel: 0121 359 6000
Fax: 0121 631 3714

Power tools
Dewalt
210 Bath Road
Slough
Berkshire SL1 3YD
Tel: 01753 572 113
Fax: 01753 572 112
www.dewalt.co.uk

Timber
C Ransford & Son
Station Street
Bishops Castle
Shropshire SY9 5AQ
Tel: 01588 638331
Fax: 01588 638853

Decking
Johnny Dobbyn
Camroon PR
Tel: 0207 4201700
Fax: 0207 4972753

Metal grill
C Downhill Steels
Unit D, Riverside Way
Uxbridge
Middlesex UB8 2YS
Tel: 01895 256681
Fax: 01895 811801

Lifting Gear Supplies Ltd
23 Anstey Lane
Leicester LE4 0FF
Tel: 0116 262 8023
Fax: 0116 2514862

Water
Hozelock Ltd
Waterslade House
Thame Road
Haddenham
Aylesbury
Bucks HP17 8JD
Tel: 01844 292022

Plants
The Herb Nursery
Thistleton
Oakham
Rutland LE15 7RE
Tel: 01572 767658
For these products look for Blooms or Country Fresh labels in your nearest garden centre. for nearest stockists tel:0800358 7689

Tendercare
Southlands Road
Denham
Uxbridge
Middlesex UB9 4HD
Tel: 01895 835544

Lighting
Paul Whittaker
AC/DC Lighting Systems Ltd
Tel: 01282 601464
Fax: 01282 692757

Massive UK Ltd
Castle Road
Eurolink Commercial Park
Sittingbourne
Kent ME19 3RN
Tel: 01795 424442
Fax: 01795 420779

The Lighting Association
Stafford Park 7
Telford
Shropshire TF3 3BQ
Tel: 01952 290905
Fax: 01952 290906

Misc
Birstall Garden Centre
Birstall Village Centre
Leicestershire LE4 4DX
Tel: 0116 267 7091
Fax: 0116 267 1318

Nipooria
85b Main Road
Gidea Park, Romford
Essex RM2 5EL
Tel: 01708 651694
www.nipooria.com

The Gadget Shop Ltd
Hesslewood Hall
Ferriby Road
Hessle HU13 0LH
Tel: 01482 626400
www.gadgetshop.com

LOUNGE LIZARDS

Flooring

Priory Steel Group Ltd
Wolverhampton Central Trading Estate
Cable Street
Wolverhampton WV2 2RL
Tel: 01902 351 001

Luxcrete Limited
Premier House, Disraeli Road
Park Royal
London NW10 7BT
Tel: 020 8965 7292

Tools

Webbs Power Tools
146 Boldmere Road
Sutton Coldfield
Birmingham B73 5UD
Tel: 0121 355 3939

Rapid Hire (UK) Limited
Intersection House
110 Birmingham Road
West Bromwich B70 6RX
Tel: 0121 500 0700

HSS Hire
350 Bloxwich Road
Walsall WS2 7BG
Tel: 01922 615181

Plantool Ltd
Millers Road
Warwick
Warwickshire CV34 5AN
Tel: 01926 402345

Skips

SITA
Waste Care Management
Montague Street
Birmingham B9 4BA
Tel: 0121 643 6430

Plants

Kinglea Plants Ltd
Shottentons Farm
Pecks Hill, Nazeing
Essex EN9 2NY
Tel: 01992 899410

Tendercare
Southlands Road
Denham, Uxbridge
Middlesex UB9 4HD
Tel: 01895 835544

Turf

Rolawn
Turf Growers Ltd
Elvington
York YO41 4XR
Tel: 01904 608 661
www.rolawn.co.uk

Ducting (Steel Plant Containers)

Fabric Air Systems
Unit 5
Burbidge Road
Bordesley Green
Birmingham
Tel: 0121 766 7707

Lighting

Brilliant UK Ltd
Hanworth Trading Estate
Hampton Road West, Feltham
Middx TW13 6DR
Tel: 020 8898 3131

Dig-It (Solar Lights)
Tel: 020 7348 7440
www.dig-it.co.uk

'Tuba' Light (Copper Tube)
McCloud Lighting
19-20 Chelsea Harbour Design Centre
London SW10
Tel: 020 7352 1533

John Cullen Lighting
Unit 24, Talina Centre
Bagleys Lane
London SW6 2BW
Tel: 020 7371 9000

The Lighting Association
Tel: 01952 290 905
Massive UK
Castle Road
Eurolink Commercial Park
Sittingbourne
Kent
Tel: 020 7352 1533

Oldham Lighting
4 Rowan Court
56 High Street
Wimbledon Village
London SW19 5EE
Tel: 020 8946 5555

Louis Poulsen Lights
Outdoor Lighting

Surrey Business Park
Weston Road, Epsom
Surrey KT17 1JG
Tel: 01372 848 818

Schott Fibre Optics (UK) Ltd
Tel: 01302 347 008
email: enquiries@schott.co.uk

Race Worldwide
3 Carters Lane
Kiln Farm
Milton Keynes MK11 3EP
Tel: 01908 561166

Flexion Optical Fibre PLC
Flexion House
Shaw Wood Business Park
Shaw Wood Way
Doncaster DN2 5TB
Tel: 01302 328282

Clifton Lighting Company
Marchdyke House
Mill Hill, Brockweir
Monmouthshire NP16 7NW
Tel: 01291 689372

P R Electrical & Alarm Wholesalers
Unit 2, Prince Road
Kings Norton Business Centre
Birmingham B30 3HB
Tel: 0121 486 1661

ESI
Electronic Security Installations
73 Frances Road
Cotteridge
Birmingham B30 3DU
Tel: 0121 247 0701

Video Projectors

Hitachi
Dukes Meadow
Millboard Road
Hall End
Buckinghamshire SL8 5XF
Tel: 01628 643 000

JVC Professional
Ullswater House
Kendal Avenue
Park Royal
London W3 OXA
Tel: 020 8896 6000
www.jvcpro.co.uk

Casio Electronics Co Ltd
Unit 6, 1000 North Circular Road
London NW2 7JD
Meter Boxes
Tel: 020 8208 9450
www.casio.co.uk

MEB, Toll End Road
Tipton
West Midlands DY4 0HH
Tel: 0121 557 2811

Mathmos
20-24 Old Street
London EC1V 9AP
Tel: 020 7549 2759
www.mathmos.co.uk

Stereo System

Nakamichi
BBG Distribution
Unit 3, Barratt Way
Tudor Road, Harrow
Middlesex, HA3 5QS
Tel: 020 8863 9117

Outdoor speakers

KEF (contact Mark Franks)
Tel: 01622 672261

Accessories

The Gadget Shop
Tel: 01482 626 400
www.gadgetshop.co.uk

Toys R Us
Oldbury
West Midlands
(Supplied all gadget dogs)
Tel: 0121 511 1331

Scots of Stow
Tel: 01285 653153

Minibar UK Ltd
468 Malton Avenue
Slough
Berkshire SL1 4QU
Tel: 0700 26464 227

Furniture

(Chrome framed chair with upholstered seat & King Chair)
Lee Longlands
224 Broad Street
Birmingham B15 1AZ
Tel: 0121 643 9101

Silver Bean Bag Chair
The Modern Garden Company
P O Box 5868
Dunmow CM6 2FB
Tel: 01279 851 900
email:info@moderngarden.co.uk
www.moderngarden.co.uk

Beanbag Cubes
The Richard Powell Home Collection
1 Sadler Road
Lincoln LN6 3RS
Tel: 01522 874 141
www.thehomecollection.co.uk

Mouldable PVC Beanbag chair
Inflate
11 Northburgh Street
London EC1V OAH
Tel: 020 7251 5453
www.inflate.co.uk

Sofa beanbag
The Sofa Bean Bag Company
Unit 6, Raynham Road Industrial Estate
Bishops Stortford
Hertfordshire CM23 5PB

Squash Seat & Lulu seat
Interiornet
Index Media Ltd
Studio 3, 436 Essex Road
London M1 3QP
Interiornet.com

The Gadget Shop Limited
Hesslewood Hall
Ferriby Road
Hessle HU13 0LH
Tel: 0800 783 8343
www.gadgetshop.com

EDIBLE EDEN

Building materials

Tarmac Group
Millfields Road
Ettingshall
Wolverhampton WV4 6JP
Tel: 01902 353522
Fax: 01902 495562

Selco Builders Merchants
Hazelwell Road
Stirchley, Birmingham
Tel: 0121 433 3355

E A Barnes & Sons Ltd
Shell Words
City Station Wharf
St John Street
Lichfield
Tel/fax: 01543 262000

Aggregate Industries
Bradstone & Charcon
Bardon Hill
Coalville
Leicestershire LE67 1TL
Tel: 01335 372222
Fax: 01335 370079

The Tile Warehouse
131 Derby Road
Stapleford
Nottingham NG9 7AS
Tel: 0115 939 0209
Fax: 0115 949 0271
tilenottingham@compuserve.com

Jewson
Station Wharf
Station Road
Stechford
Birmingham B33 9AF
Tel: 0121 783 2287

Adey Steel
8 Sparrow Hill
Loughborough
Leicestershire LE11 1BT
Tel: 01509 556677
Fax: 01509 828622

Millington Building Materials
188 Litchfield Road
Four Oaks
Sutton Coldfield
West Mids B74 2TX
Tel: 0121 308 9500
Fax: 0121 308 6753

Sto Ltd
Unit 4
The Ringway Centre
Edison Road
Basingstoke RG21 6YH
Tel: 01256 332770

Railway Sleepers

C Ransford & Son
Station Street
Bishops Castle
Shropshire SY9 5AQ
Tel: 01588 638331
Fax: 01588 638853

Power Tools

Dewalt
210 Bath Road
Slough
Berkshire SL1 3YD
Tel 01753 572 113
Fax 01753 572 112
www.dewalt.co.uk

Tool Hire

Rodger Webb hirecentres.com
Tel: 0800 834360

SGB Hire Plus
81 Liverpool Street
Bordesley
Birmingham B9 4DS
Tel: 0121 753 2266
Fax: 0121 753 1166

Rapid Hire
Unit 34
Kelvin Way Trading Estate
Kelvin Way
West Bromwich B70 7TP
Tel: 0121 500 5474

Turf

Rolawn (Turf Growers) Ltd
Box Trees Farm
Stratford Road
Hockley Heath
Solihull B94 6EA
Tel: 01564 784064
Fax: 01564 784049

Organic materials

Border Aggregates Ltd
Scotland Road
Carnforth
Lancashire LA5 9JZ
Tel: 01524 732977
Fax: 01524 720102

Organic Plus
14 Startforth Park
Barnard Castle
Co Durham DL12 9AL
Tel: 0845 1274973
www.organic-plus.co.uk

Pennine Organic Fertilizers Ltd
Square Lane
Catforth
Preston PR4 OHQ
Tel: 01772 690261
www.pennine-organic.co.uk

Wiggly Wigglers
Lower Blakemore
Herefordshire HR2 9PX
Tel: 0800 216990
www.wigglywigglers.co.uk

Water

Hozelock Ltd
Waterslade House
Thame Road
Haddenham
Aylesbury
Bucks HP17 8JD
Tel: 01844 292002

Furniture

Trannon Furniture
Chilhampton Fram
Wilton
Salisbury SP2 0AB
Tel: 01722 744 577
Fax: 01722 744 477

Habitat UK
88-91 New Street
Birmingham B2 4HS
Tel: 0121 643 5647

Bouchon Ltd
309 Metrostore
5-10 Eastman Road
London W3 7YG
Tel: 020 8740 9744
Fax: 020 8749 7566
email: mailorder@bouchon.co.uk

Fabric

Russell and Chappel Ltd
68 Druary Lane WC2B 5SP
Tel: 020 7836 7521

Skips

EA Barnes & Sons Ltd
Shell Works
City station Wharf
St John's Street
Litchfiels
Staffordshire WS14 9DZ
Tel: 01543 262000

Plants

Tendercare Nurseries Ltd
Southlands Road, Denham,
Uxbridge,
Middlesex UB94HD
Tel: 01895 835544

Jekka's Herb Farm
Rose Cottage, Shellards Lane,
Alveston, Bristol BS35 3SY
Tel. 01454 418878

JAPAN

Railway Sleepers

T. Ward Shipping Ltd
3 St John's Place
Leith
Edinburgh EH6 7EL
Tel: 0131 554 1231

Recycled Materials

'George Chair' (reclaimed timber)
Pendlewood
4 Osbourne Road
Salford M6 8JE
Tel: 0161 789 4441

Bird Table (reclaimed timber)
The Pathway Workshop
Dunnock Way
Blackbird Leys
Oxford OX4 5EX
Tel: 01865 714111

Recycled Planters and Woodchip
distributed by:
Leisuregrow Products
WRM Logistics Centre
Knowle Piece
Wilbury Way, Hitchin
Herts SG4 OTY
Tel: 01462 451700
Fax: 01462 450039
www.leisuregrow.co.uk

'Epoch' Recycled Planter
EPP (Environmental Polymer
Products)
Bold Industrial Park
Neills Road, Bold
St Helens
Merseyside WA9 4TU
Tel: 01744 810001

Recycled Products Ltd
Lindsey house
Caenby Corner Estate
Hemswell Cliff
Gainsborough
Lincolnshire DN21 5TH
Tel: 01427 668822

Woodlands Farm Nursery &
Reclamation
The Green, Wood Street Village
Nr. Guildford
Surrey GU3 3DU
Tel: 01483 235536
www.salvoweb.co.uk

Garden Sculptures

The Birmingham Botanical Gardens
and Glasshouses
Westbourne Road
Edgbaston
Birmingham B15 3TR
Tel:0121 454 1860

Ann Ford
Sculpture Garden & Studio
Eggmoor Lane Cottage
Chardstock, Axminster
Devon EX13 7BP
Tel: 01460 221193
email:ann@eggmoor.freeserve.co.uk
www.glider.demon.co.uk/annford

Peter Hayes
2 Cleveland Bridge
Bath BA1 5DH
Tel: 01225 466215
email:@compuserve.com
www.peterhayes-cerramics.uk.com

Big Art
36 Oxford Street
Grantham
Lincolnshire NG31 6HQ
Tel: 01476 569 115
www.bigart.co.uk

Jonathan Stamper
High Head Farm
Ivegill
Carlisle CA4 0PJ

Brian Hollingworth
11 Clumber Avenue
Mapperley Plains
Nottingham NG3 5JY
Tel: 0115 9262430
www.animal-sculpture.co.uk

The Gnome Reserve
West Putford
near Bradworthy
North Devon EX22 7XE
Tel: 01409 241435

Stephen Vince
Bylaugh Hall
Bylaugh Park
Dereham
Norfolk NR20 4RL
Tel: 01362 688343

Gardd Geltaidd (The Celtic Garden)
Bron Meillion
Tregeiriog, Llangollen
Wales LL20 7HT
Tel: 01691 600259
e-mail: celticgarden@freeuk.com
www.celticgarden.freeuk.com

Stone & Water Ltd.
Stapleford Industrial Estate
Saxby Road (Nr. Saxby)
Melton Mowbray
Leicester LE14 2SB
Tel: 01572 787788
www.stoneandwater.co.uk

Dig it (online) plc
Tel: 020 7348 7440
www.dig-it.co.uk

Ben May
Tel: 01805 622214
mushrooms@forestcrafts.co.uk
www.forestcrafts.co.uk

McCord - Design By Mail
Tel: 0870 908 7005
www.emccord.com

Building Materials

Harvey Building Supplies
57 Fishwives Causeway
East Telferton
Edinburgh EH7 6GH
Tel: 0131 468 1717

SR Hire Centres
15/19 West Bowling Green Street
Leith
Edinburgh EH6 5PQ
Tel: 0131 555 3500

Thistle Timber & Building Supplies Limited
20 The Wisp
Edinburgh EH16 4SQ
Tel: 0131 669 4125

Edinburgh Hire Centre
6 Falco Road West
Edinburgh EH10 4AQ
Tel: 0131 447 8782

Frontier Forestry Ltd
Tel: 0786 777 8936

Keyline Builders Merchant
1 Baltic Street
Leith
Edinburgh EH6 7BR
Tel: 0131 519 5000

Plants

R & B Nursery Ltd
Melville Nursery
Lasswade
Midlothian EH18 1AZ
Tel: 0131 663 1944

East Neuk Water Garden Centre
Crail
Fife
Tel: 01333 450 530

SEA VIEW

Building materials

Thistle Timber & Building Supplies Ltd
20 The Wisp
Edinburgh EH16 4SQ
Tel: 0131 669 4125
Fax: 0131 669 8774

Jewson Ltd
58 Craigentinny Ave
Midlothian EH6 7RD
Tel: 0131 554 1144

The Outdoor Decking Company
Mortimer House
46 Sheen Lane
London
SW14 8LP
Tel: 020 8876 8464
Fax: 020 8878 8687

Armourcoat Ltd
Morewood Close
London Road
Sevenoaks
Kent DA12 2AP
armourcoat.co.uk
Tel: 01732 460668

Tarmac Northern Ltd
Strathclyde Business Park

PO Box 8720
Belshill
Glasgow ML4 3WB
Tel: 01698 575500

Alumasc Exterior Building
Products Ltd
White House Works
Bold Road
Sutton
St. Helens
Merseyside WA9 4JG
Tel: 01744 648 400

Sto Ltd
Unit 4
The Ringway Centre
Edison Road
Basingstoke
RG21 6YH
Tel: 01256 332770

Zydeco
http://www.zydeco.co.uk
mail@zydeco.demon.co.uk
Fax: 01705 423755

Decramace Ltd
Mount Sion Road
Radcliffe
Manchester M26 3SJ
Tel: 0161 724 5867

Alsecco (UK) Ltd
Meaford Power Station
Meaford, Stone
Staffordshire ST15 0UA
Tel: 01782 374 066
www.alsecco.co.uk

Reclaimed materials

Hargreaves Reclaimed flooring
26 Castle Road
Bankside Industrial Estate
Falkirk FK2 7XX
Tel 01324 611152
Fax 01324 633888

Tiling

Smith and Wareham
Tile Merchants
Eastgate Street
Bury St Edmunds
Suffolk IP33 1YQ
Tel: 01284 704 188
www.smithandwareham.co.uk

Roman Mosaic Ltd
Bloomfield Road
Tipton
West Midlands DY4 9ES
Tel: 0121 520 8151
sales@romanmosaic.co.uk

Power Tools

Dewalt
210 Bath Road
Slough
Berkshire SL1 3YD
Tel: 01753 572 113
Fax: 01753 572 112
www.dewalt.co.uk

Martin Plant Hire
Kensington House
227 Sauchiehall St
Glasgow G2 3EX
Tel: 0141 332 5197
Fax: 0141 332 6875

Plants

Melville Nurseries
Lasswade
Midlothian EH18 1AZ
Tel: 0131 663 1944

Rolawn (Turf Growers) Ltd
Elvington
York YO14 4XR
Tel: 01904 608661
Fax: 01904 608272

Depot used:
13 East Mains Holding
Ingliston
Newbridge
Edinburgh EH28 8NB
Tel: 0131 335 3164

Patio Heaters

Rusco Outdoor Furniture
Little Faringdon Mill
Lechdale
Gloucestershire GL7 3QQ
Tel: 01367 252367

Calor Gas Direct
Athena Drive
Tachbrook Park
Warwick CV34 6RL
Tel: 0800 662 663

AW Stokes & Son (Drums) Ltd
Hall Street
West Bromwich
West Midlands B70 7DN
Tel: 0121 553 1713

index

Page numbers in italic refer to the illustrations

This book is published to accompany the television series *Planet Patio,* broadcast in May 2001.

Executive producers: Rachel Innes-Lumsden and Franny Moyle
Series producer: Andy Francis

Published by BBC Worldwide Ltd, Woodlands, 80 Wood Lane, London W12 0TT

First published 2001

BBC Worldwide would like to thank the following for providing photographs and permission to reproduce copyright material. While every effort has been made to trace and acknowledge all copyright holders, we would like to apologize should there have been any errors or omissions.
Abbreviations: (t) top, (b) bottom, (c) centre, (l) left, (r) right.
Advertising archives p21(t), p39(br); Indian Ocean (t), Modern Garden Company (c & b), p34, BBC *The Good Life* p66; *BBC Gardener's World* Magazine p45(l&r), p61(r); Birstall Garden Centre P46(bc); Garden Matters Picture Library p45(cl&cr); Harpur Garden Library p20, p51, p87; Inflate Ltd p63(cl); Robin Matthews/BBC Worldwide p56(c&r), p61(cl); Modern Garden Co p62(tl); Ocean Ltd p46(bl); Sunshine Lifestyle Products Ltd p46(br).

ISBN 0 563 53712 4

Commissioning Editor: Nicky Copeland Project Editor: Helena Caldon
Art Direction and Design: Lisa Pettibone Illustrations: Ann Ramsbottom
Picture Research: Bea Thomas

Set in Meta Plus and Helvetica Rounded
Printed and bound in France by Imprimerie Pollina s.a. n° L82652
Colour separations by Kestrel Digital Colour Ltd, Chelmsford, Essex